Going from
C to C++

Going from
C to C++

Robert J. Traister

Robert J. Traister & Associates
Front Royal, Virginia

Academic Press Professional
A Division of Harcourt Brace & Company

Boston   San Diego   New York
London   Sydney   Tokyo   Toronto

ACADEMIC PRESS PROFESSIONAL
955 Massachusetts Avenue, Cambridge, MA 02139

An Imprint of ACADEMIC PRESS, INC.
A Division of HARCOURT BRACE & COMPANY

United Kingdom Edition published by
ACADEMIC PRESS LIMITED
24-28 Oval Road, London NW1 7DX

Library of Congress Cataloging-in-Publication Data

Traister, Robert J.
        Going from C to C++ / Robert J. Traister.
            p.   cm.
        Includes index.
        ISBN 0-12-697412-8
        I. C (Computer program language)   2. C++ (Computer program
language) I. Title.
        QA76.73.C153T74   1993
        005.13'3—dc20   92-47470
                                                         CIP

Printed in the United States of America
93 94 95 96 97 98   EB   9 8 7 6 5 4 3 2 1

This book is dedicated to my dear friend and "links" nemesis David Nuttall Crump, Jr., his lovely wife Kimberly, and the children: Oliver, Joshua, Alyssa, Tyler, and Evan.

Contents

Preface

A decade ago, C was a language that was little known outside of the arena of the highly professional systems programmer. Its advantages were appreciated by this small group of individuals, but there was a tendency for them to be rather secretive about their excursions into C. At this time, the ability to program in C was a status symbol, one that many programmers were not willing to lose to the possibility of C's becoming the programming language of the masses.

Also a decade ago, this author was completing a book titled *Going From Basic to C* for a large publisher. Coming from a BASIC language background, it was my belief that many who programmed in this language might be tempted to make the switch to C if only they could get some good, understandable information about this language. One must remember that during the first years of the 1980s, C language tutorials were mostly nonexistent. Certainly, there was Kernighan and Ritchie's *The C Programming Language,* but this was not a tutorial by their own admission. It was my hope to produce a definitive work that would hold the BASIC programmer's hand while taking him or her into the initially frightening realm of C. When the manuscript was completed, the publisher sent it out immediately to three reviewers who were professional C programmers. That's when the roof fell in!

"This author doesn't realize that C cannot be taught within a framework of BASIC," they said. Going further, they avowed, "A BASIC programmer must forget everything he or she has learned about BASIC in order to learn C. Knowledge of BASIC will simply hinder the serious programmer who is learning C." In short, all three wondered who this young upstart was, this barbarian who was trying to infiltrate the "priesthood" that called itself the C Programming Community.

Fortunately, I stood by my guns with an editor who, for some reason, had great faith in me. The book was published, and it was an immediate success. To date, it has been translated into thirteen foreign languages including Japanese, Russian, and Arabic. And it still enjoys some moderate success after more than ten years of being in print.

Today, I'm hearing similar (misguided) comments about C++. "This is an object-oriented language, not procedural-based (as is ANSI C). The best thing to do is to learn to program all over again. After all, it's the wave of the future!"

If you're like me, you don't appreciate being told that all of the hard work you have done to become proficient at programming in C has been wasted.

Going From C to C++ is a book designed to do just what its title implies. Each reader is encouraged to bring all of his or her knowledge of ANSI C along on this journey. Transitioning to C++ is not as hard as some think (or want you to think). C++ is a logical evolution that uses all of your C language knowledge and allows you, almost immediately, to put it to more powerful uses.

Typical books on C++ programming and the object-oriented approach fall into two categories. The first offers in-depth treatises on object-oriented programming by supplying dull, endless verbiage accompanied by lengthy charts showing family trees, company employee/management structures, breeder charts of dog/cat lineage, and even bacterial growth reports. This is supposed to explain in intimate detail the concept of object-oriented programming?

The second approach is a conversational breeze-through of the concept, allowing the author's jovial personality to show through. Typically, it's accompanied by such phrases and discussion headers as "morphing a task," "object-oriented programming, a CLASS act," and the omnipresent "if you don't understand the full concept at this point, don't worry about it. It'll come to you in time." Unfortunately, the time is far longer than most students of a new language can tolerate or, much less, desire.

The discussions in this book are based upon many grueling hours of hands-on programming using the conventions of the C++ language. This was a process of trial and error, which for most of us is the method whereby we learn the most. What there is of this author's jovial personality will not shine through like some welcome beacon and there will be no endless charts on yeast growth rates.

The author's only claim to fame is in having had reasonable success in taking programmers who are proficient in one language into a new language. This has been done by drawing as many references to the known language as possible while still providing a good tutorial advantage. One most important aspect of this process is the author's ability "never to forget what he didn't know." This statement is not an attempt to be cute, but actually describes the process by which this book has been written. Ignorance is very important and we are all ignorant when we tackle the learning of a new language.

Unfortunately, many teachers of a new language soon consider themselves to be experts and forget their former ignorance and frustrations of not knowing when they attempt to teach. Again, this author retains a very sharp memory of his ignorance when first attempting to learn C++. He remembers what he didn't know, and he remembers the steps he took to overcome this lack. These efforts are presented here step-by-step and with an understanding of the frustrations that accompany the journey from C to C++.

This text will constantly reference the ANSI C language in explaining the new tools offered by C++. Object-oriented programming? Chances are you have been writing applications with objects in mind for a long time. You just didn't know you were doing it. In any event, this book will introduce you to the ins and outs of C++ within a framework of ANSI C, the language you currently know best. As your study continues, you will gradually begin to think in C++, and eventually, you will develop an object-oriented approach to many programming challenges.

Don't leave behind what you have already learned. Bring it along with you, and you will learn C++ that much faster.

— Robert J. Traister

Acknowledgments

The author wishes to thank Borland International, Incorporated for the invaluable assistance this company has provided in researching materials for this text. All program examples were written and compiled using Borland C++, Turbo C++ for DOS, and Turbo C++ for Windows. The author is especially grateful to Publishing Relations Manager, Nan Borreson, for her personal attention in quickly providing the resources necessary for this and numerous other projects designed to offer powerful programming capabilities to a wide range of readers.

Certain text portions and program examples in this book have been reprinted from the seminar materials, C++ Principles and Applications for ANSI C Programmers, copyright © 1990 by Robert J. Traister & Associates.

Chapter 1
++++++++++++++
Going from C to C++:
A Journey of Understanding

"C++, an object-oriented superset of the C programming language, is touted as the most beneficial language ever developed for the microcomputer, perhaps for all types of computers."

It is not unusual that C++ should be referred to in such a manner, for the C programming language was similarly described, especially in regard to use on modern microcomputers. Such statements are certainly arguable, but it is unrefuted that C and C++ have served and are serving the programming community in a very efficient manner.

The discussions in this book assume that the reader is knowledgeable and has the ability to program efficiently in C, or ANSI C as it is most accurately called today. But what is C++?

C++ is a superset of the C programming language. With very few exceptions, any code that has been written in ANSI C will compile and execute as expected under a C++ compiler. Therefore, C++ is, indeed, the entire C programming language. However, added to the ANSI C module are additional functions, operators, and most important, capabilities that are designed to allow the traditional C language to facilitate an object-oriented programming mode. This is in addition to the normal procedural-based operational personality of original ANSI C. In other words, a C++ compiler can be used to write standard ANSI C code or to move into the realm of object-oriented programming by incorporating the C++ additions.

Terminology is a major stumbling block to ANSI C programmers who are entering the C++ object-oriented environment for the first time. All ANSI C programs will compile and run in a normal fashion under C++. Therefore, understanding the object-oriented approach and the aspects of C++ that are used (and that are different from an ANSI C approach) is the main hurdle that must be overcome in the journey to efficient C++ programming. To be more specific, efficient C++ programming is the same as efficient object-oriented programming using this language.

1

Even at this early point in the discussion, the biggest terminology stumbling block has been used many times and without a clear definition. What is object-oriented programming? What does it mean? How does it work? Is it limited only to C++? The questions go on ad infinitum.

Also, the textbook definitions of object-oriented programming seem to hurt more than they help. For that matter, object-oriented programmers differ (argue incessantly) over the true definition of their art.

Object-Oriented Programming

Object-oriented programming (OOP) is the main reason for the development of the C++ language. C++ is a superset of the ANSI C programming language that allows for an OOP style, if desired. If not, the programmer may use C++ in the exact manner that he or she used ANSI C. Many programming tasks are best handled in an object-oriented manner, while other tasks are more suited to a procedural-based format. However, as the programmer moves more into the realm of OOP, he or she will find that this approach is the one first considered (and preferred) for all tasks.

Programmers moving from C to C++ normally ease into OOP with their first source code offerings taking on some of the characteristics of each programming style or method. As experience increases, the source code gradually conforms to strict OOP approaches.

But what is OOP? How does it differ from the procedural approach the programmer has been accustomed to using under ANSI C?

The Object

First, it is necessary to consider the definition of the word *object*. An object is a thing, a unique thing with its own characteristics of appearance and/or behavior. It is different from other types of objects. For instance, an automobile is an object. It is different from a dog. The transmission in an automobile can be replaced, but we cannot replace the transmission in a dog. Now, an automobile is comprised of other types of objects: a transmission, a motor, an electric system, etc. Therefore, the automobile object derives its personality from other components that, in themselves, are made from still other objects.

Taking this a step farther, a truck is an object and a car is another type of object. They are different, but they could both be classed as automobiles. We might arrive at one encompassing object classified as

AUTOMOBILE. However, part of the makeup of this object is two discrete objects. Both the truck and the car contain a transmission and a motor along with a bevy of additional, related components.

The gist of this discussion is that objects are rather complex in most instances, being comprised of other components that, in themselves, are objects. However, we don't need to be experts on the internal combustion engine or transmissions to operate an automobile. The makeup and operation of these components is not necessary to the proper operation of the automobile. Therefore, they may not even be considered by the driver.

Returning to computer programming, an object is an entity that has certain characteristics. It is not necessary for the user to know the mechanics behind the production of these characteristics, only that they are available. In other words, the user does not need to know the intimate workings of the object in order to drive it.

In this case, the user and the programmer are one and the same. But how can this be if the programmer must write the code that determines the characteristics of the object? The answer to this often-asked question is that the programmer must build each of the characteristics into an object just like a mechanic builds an automobile transmission. However, after it is built, it can be ignored, and the finished product, the object, is used without regard to what it actually contains. This will still be a bit confusing, but let's consider a common ANSI C function.

The printf() function is used to display formatted data on the monitor screen. Do you know how it works? Are you intimately familiar with the source code that went into the writing of this function? Probably not. Why bother? All that should be of concern is learning the characteristics of this function. It is necessary only to know what it requires in the form of arguments and what it does based on these arguments. When it comes to displaying information on the screen with printf(), it's not necessary to know how it does it, only that it does!

The printf() function is not an object in the true sense of OOP, but it does serve as an excellent example (along with every other ANSI C function) of the so-called black box approach most programmers use every programming day. Even when the programmer writes custom functions to address some task, the internals of these functions often become lost in the programmer's mind, overshadowed by the characteristics or personality such a function assumes in actual operation.

However, there is a very big difference between true objects and traditional entities such as functions, files, and records that inhabit the procedural-based language environment found in ANSI C.

The problem with these non-objects is that they are transparent. This means that if a program can access them at all, it can access everything about them. There are no restrictions. For instance, an int variable can be addressed by many different functions. The value in that variable can be altered by direct assignments, functions, and many other ways. There is no limited access to the contents of that variable. For this reason, the int variable cannot be classified as a true object in OOP terminology.

In the real world, objects have a personality that is determined by things most persons cannot often see or access. This means that what can be seen of them is not all there is. Objects in OOP are similar in that they have a visible outer form, and they have an inner structure and response characteristics that cannot be directly manipulated from the outside.

When dealing with computers, programmers are limited to a very few basic entities that can be manipulated, including variables, constants, data records, etc. All of these are numeric, at least as they are viewed by the computer. It is from these few components that the OOP programmer builds unique objects with personalities. Objects of this type often accept assignments, But they cannot be assigned internal values using (for instance) the intrinsic assignment operator (=).

Rather, each object has its own assignment characteristic. Objects often display internal information on the monitor screen, but this cannot be done using printf(). The personality of such an object includes a feature that causes some internal value to be displayed. That is one of the object's characteristics. Another object may not have the same characteristic. All objects are different, discrete entities.

The short and long of it involves an object that is self-supporting. It contains all of the necessary characteristics to make assignments to itself, display itself, and internally manipulate data in a manner that is unique to this object and to no other. Most important is the fact that the object contents cannot be manipulated by an entity other than the object, proper. The internal data are hidden from any program in which the object is made a part, just like the gears in a transmission are hidden from the person driving the automobile.

OOP objects contain not only data, but also methods (member-functions) for manipulating the data. Code and data can be tightly bound so that nothing outside the object has direct access to the data, and the only way to change the characteristics or action of the object is to send a message to the object. In other instances, it is advantageous to make some or all of the object data available to other program entities. The programmer who designs the object makes the choices to designate how private or public an object will be.

Objects that are very private act like black boxes. They have a message-passing interface to the rest of the program, and once they are properly coded, they are highly resistant to mistakes in other parts of the program. When they receive a valid message, they respond in a predictable manner. Objects have another important characteristic: They can be closely related to each other just like a car is related to a truck and vice versa.

Admittedly, most of the discussion about objects to this point has not really added greatly to the understanding of just what they are. However, this preface is necessary for the reader to firmly grasp the idea that, for the most part, an object is a self-contained entity. It makes its own provisions for assigning internal data members and for manipulating and displaying those data. Generally, program objects do not and will not react to outside entities such as intrinsic (built-in) functions statements, etc. The program that uses the object cannot change the personality of the object. This is fixed and is a part of the object's personality.

OOP involves two major steps. First, it is necessary to design the object. This means that the programmer must decide exactly what the object is to do and how it is to behave. The second aspect is to use the object (often combined with the operation of other objects) to accomplish a task. Objects, once built, can be used in many different programs to address tasks they were designed to handle.

A Practical Example

The best way to explain OOP at this point in the discussion is to use an ANSI C program concept and then compare it with the equivalent OOP approach. Imagine the need to design a pop-up window function, one that will produce a pop-up window on the screen when called. This also necessitates designing another function that will remove the pop-up window when it is no longer needed. A pop-up window is one that is written over the current screen contents. When it is removed (popped down), the original screen contents reappear undisturbed.

To do this, it is necessary to design the popup() function so that it can be handed arguments that determine the x, y coordinates of the left upper edge of the window and the x, y coordinates of the lower right edge. Other arguments might be included to determine the background color of the window and the text write color.

When popup() is executed, the function must first save the portion of the screen that is to be overwritten by the pop-up window. When this is done, the window can then be written. At this point, popup() has done its job and this function is exited. The prototype for this function might resemble the following example.

```
popup(lx, ly, rx, ry, bgc, tc, *oldscreen, *textstring);
```

where lx and ly are the x, y coordinate values of the upper left window edge; rx and ry are the right edge coordinates; bgc is the window background color; tc is the text color; *oldscreen is a pointer to an array that contains the byte contents of the original screen that is to be overwritten by the window; and *textstring is a pointer to the string that is to be written in the window.

Now that the pop-up window has been written, it is necessary to consider how it is to be removed. Remember, the popup() function really can't remove the window, since the length of time it must remain on the screen and the operations that must take place while it is there are variable from program to program. Therefore, a function named popdown() might be written that would be prototyped in the following manner.

```
popdown(lx, ly, rx, ry, *oldscreen);
```

The argument parameters are the same as those used with popup() except that the background and text color arguments along with the textstring argument are unnecessary.

This function would calculate the starting and ending write positions on the screen and simply write the bytes contained in *oldscreen over the screen position where the pop-up window currently resides. The end effect is that of a window that pops up over the current screen contents and then disappears (when popdown() is executed), leaving the original screen contents intact.

Problem: If several pop-up windows are active at once, it is necessary to declare a different textstring and oldscreen array for each. Naturally, these arrays must be given different names. Also, additional variables must be named to contain all of the other arguments for each pop-up window that is to be displayed. Ten windows will require ten different variable sets for each of the functions. There would be a very real possibility of getting this many variables confused and writing a window in a wrong location, or worse, writing a window at one location and trying to pop it down at another.

Using an OOP approach, there would be a single object type. Call it POP for the sake of this discussion. This object type would have the characteristics of both of the above functions. This object has certain characteristics called METHODs, which determine how the object type will behave.

Within a C++ program, several object variables would be declared as shown below.

```
POP window1, window2, window3;
```

This statement names three objects of type POP. Each of the objects has the same characteristics of the other. However, they are all discrete objects of type POP.

Now, let's assume that POP object window1 is to be used to write a pop-up window with the left corner at coordinate 100, 150 and the right lower corner at coordinate 200, 250. The text string to be written in this window is "Popup Window1 Example", and it is to appear in a window with a background color of 1 and a text color of 3. This might be handed to the object in the following manner.

```
window1.assign(100, 150, 200, 250, 1, 3, "Popup Window1 Example");
```

As before, it is necessary to provide the parameters for a write to the object. This example uses constants, but variables would serve as well. Notice, however, that the oldscreen parameter is not included, as this object type would automatically allocate storage internally for the storage of the old screen based upon the left and right screen coordinates.

This example shows that a METHOD of the POP object type called **assign** has been used to assign these values to the internal data structure of the object. How does this method accomplish this assignment? The answer will be presented in detail later in this text, but the correct answer is "Who cares?" It is enough to know that the method named assign will make the necessary assignments. It is not necessary (at this point) to know how it does it, since it is assumed that POP is an object that has been previously built. All that is left is to use that object.

Now that all of the parameters have been assigned, the window can be popped up in the following manner.

```
window1.up();
```

This example reveals the name of another method that is a part of this object's personality. Arbitrarily named **up()**, this method causes the current contents of the screen where the window is to be written to be stored in an internal array. Next, the window appears on the screen.

To this point, the POP object does not seem to be too different from the popup() function discussed earlier. However, the differences begin to reveal themselves when the window is to be popped down. How is this done and what arguments are required? It's really quite simple, as the following statement shows.

```
window1.down();
```

That's all there is to it. There are no arguments, since all of the necessary data are already contained within the window1 object. The window will be overwritten by the original screen data stored in the object, which include the x, y coordinates and the stored original screen contents.

All of this put together yields an object type that is unique. There is no other data type that performs exactly as this one. Furthermore, the other objects of type POP (window2 and window3) can be used to cause other windows to pop-up. Each window becomes an object, controlled by its methods. This is true OOP. The object assigns itself in its own special way and behaves according to its personality. The object-oriented approach is far better for the assigned task of pop-up windows generation that the procedural-based ANSI C approach.

To avoid confusion, don't be misled into thinking that assign(), up(), and down() are some type of special, intrinsic functions or methods used with OOP approaches. These are all programmer-designed and programmer-named methods that could just as easily have been given any other name. The actual code used for these methods to perform their operations is straightforward, and some of it closely resembles the code that would be used in an ANSI C function that performed similar operations. However, all of these capabilities are combined into one object and not spread among four or five discrete functions as would be the case in an ANSI C implementation.

The object of type POP is unique. It cannot be assigned by any intrinsic C or C++ function or operator. It cannot be displayed by any C or C++ function such as printf(). Its abilities (and limitations) are entirely internal.

The POP object must have some sort of storage set aside for containing the values handed it using the assign() method. How can we take a look at these? We can't. In most objects, there is no way that a program can delve into the inner workings or be used in any way to modify internal values. Certainly, a programmer can view the source code that makes up the object, but the PROGRAM cannot do this unless given special permission, which will be discussed in a later chapter.

To summarize in object-oriented terminology, window1, window2, and window3 in the above examples are discrete objects of type POP. All of the objects have the same operational characteristics, because they are of the same type, just as it might be said that all number 10 wash buckets are alike. However, each object may be put to a different use, depending upon (in this case) the location, color, and text data that are assigned. All data, regardless of actual value, are stored, manipulated, and displayed in the same manner, just as a number 10 wash bucket may hold water, gasoline, or maple syrup. The personality of the wash bucket is one of containment. The personality of the POP object type is one of display and erasure.

Now that a very general concept of the object-oriented approach has been provided, the next logical question concerns how to build objects. True objects simply cannot be made using the ANSI C language. The capability is just not there. To enter the realm of OOP, it is necessary to use C++, which offers everything ANSI C does plus the ability to use relatively familiar code structures in an object-oriented manner.

C++ offers many additions to ANSI C that will be of immediate benefit to the ANSI C programmer and that will not change your current programming style. The great majority of these features are a welcome addition to ANSI C and are absolutely essential to OOP.

It is by combining your current knowledge of ANSI C programming with the enhanced capabilities of C++ that true objects may be built and used to address an endless array of programming tasks.

Using the pop-up window example, it should be stressed that much of the code that would be used in this application under ANSI C would be duplicated in a C++ object, in modified form. However, the code is encapsulated and made private. Individual C++ programming elements are not so very different from ANSI C elements. However, the methods by which code is combined, encapsulated, and placed in a limited access category is very different from those methods to which ANSI C programmers are accustomed. Fortunately, many parallels can be made directly with ANSI C, and these likenesses will be used to make a smooth transition from C to C++.

Summary

C++ is an enhancement of the original ANSI C language, a superset that adds many features designed especially to allow for an OOP approach. At the same time, C++ supports all (with few exceptions) of the ANSI C conventions. Therefore, procedural-based ANSI C code will still compile and execute in a normal fashion.

The only reason to switch to C++ is to enter the realm of OOP. This type of programming architecture offers a more natural approach to problem solving within the computer environment. OOP attempts to mimic the manner in which human beings view and manipulate objects in the real world. While programmers who are firmly fixed in a procedural-based language may not agree, OOP offers an easier approach to task management because it is more in line with the way humans naturally tend to relate to and address tasks.

Once a full understanding of the OOP approach is grasped by the reader, the transition from procedural-based ANSI C to object-oriented C++ will be a natural and welcome one.

Chapter 2
++++++++++++++
C++ I/O Streams

One of the powerful additions to the original C programming language that is offered by C++ is a new input/output (I/O) streaming system. This greatly enhances I/O operations without having to resort to large functions and highly complex format controls as is necessarily the case when programming in ANSI C. Typically, the printf() function is used for output to the monitor screen and scanf() is called for input from the keyboard.

A *stream* is simply a reference to any flow of data from a producer to a consumer. Using C++ programming terminology, the producer is called the *source* and the consumer is the *sink*. Terms such as *getting, putting, fetching, storing, reading,* and *writing* are used when referencing the inputting of characters from a source or the outputting of characters to a sink.

The discussions that follow will introduce the ANSI C programmer to C++ I/O streams in a manner that builds on his or her knowledge of C language. The transition to using I/O streams in C++ is an easy method of reading and writing data that usually presents no major difficulties to the ANSI C programmer. In fact, streaming is a more natural method of reading and writing data. With this in mind, C++ I/O streams do not require a whole rethinking of the screen write/keyboard scan processes currently found in ANSI C. C++ I/O streams offer a far easier method of accomplishing such operations in a logical manner that is immediately accepted and understood by the ANSI C programmer.

Most professional programmers think of I/O as a flow of data from the program to a target known as the sink or from a source to the program. For instance, when data are read from disk, the disk file becomes the source. When data are written to a disk file, the file becomes the sink.

ANSI C programmers tend to think of the stdio.h header file as a black box in that it provides all of the mechanisms for I/O operations. Just as it is unnecessary to have intimate knowledge of the thermodynamics of the internal combustion engine in order to drive an automobile, one does not have to know every aspect of stdio.h to perform I/O operations. It is only necessary to learn how these mechanisms are used. This relates to an earlier discussion on C++ objects. It's not necessary to know how an object does something. It's only important to know what it can do. The same applies to stdio.h.

Using stdio.h, several facilities are placed at the programmer's disposal. This header file establishes a buffer to contain data, a structure or file object to contain information about the stream, and the standard library routines that use the buffer and the file object.

C++ also supports I/O under the auspices of stdio.h, since C++ embraces the entire content of the original ANSI C language. However, the most efficient way of handling these same operations is via IOSTREAM.H, a header file that is new to the ANSI C programmer. C++ is an object-oriented language, and IOSTREAM.H uses classes (as opposed to structures in C) to provide the enhanced I/O capabilities provided by this new type of stream.

It is important to understand that IOSTREAM.H sets up **class objects** for I/O operations. For the time being, these classes may be thought of as elements of IOSTREAM.H that are interrelated. Later, a full understanding of classes will be discussed. In shorthand form, data that are committed to a class become an object with its own personality, capabilities, and limitations.

Streambuf

One of the classes established in IOSTREAM.H is named streambuf. An object of this class is equivalent to the I/O buffer in stdio.h. However, a streambuf object not only stores data, but also provides the vital implements to move data characters in and out of the buffer. In addition, it can flush the buffer and even open and close a disk file if the I/O involves disk file operations.

IOS

All stream classes contained in iostream.h are derived from a base class named **ios**. This class is similar to the FILE object in stdio.h. The main purpose of this class is to keep track of the stream status, monitoring the flow of data from the source to the sink. A major purpose of this class is error detection and the reporting of error conditions. It also contains the address of the streambuf object. The ios class is the base class for two other classes that perform the actual I/O operations. A later chapter on C++ classes will explain this statement in more detail, but for now, it is enough to know that all I/O operations performed using iostream.h receive information through or transmit information through this class. Envision ios as a class through which all I/O operations are filtered. The ios class creates two additional classes that are named istream and ostream for input-stream and output-stream. From ios, istream and ostream are created. The combination of the two provides full access to input and output streams.

The iostream.h header file contains all declarations for the four C++ streams, which are named **cin**, **cout**, **cerr**, and **clog**. The cin stream is of type istream. The other three streams are of type ostream. The chart below shows this breakdown.

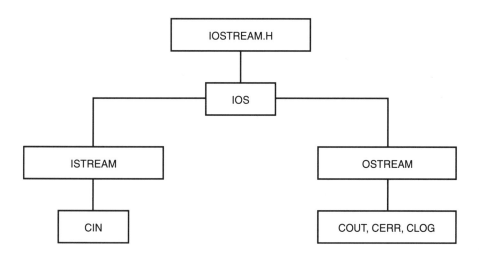

In this representation, CIN is the input stream, while COUT, CERR, and CLOG are output streams. CERR is line buffered and CLOG is the fully buffered version of CERR. Using the stdio.h header file streams as a comparison, cin matches with stdin, cout with stdout, cerr with stderr, and clog with a fully buffered stderr.

The ANSI C programmer will obtain a better grasp of iostream.h by comparing its facilities with those in stdio.h. Just as iostream.h is a complex header file with several different major components, the same applies to stdio.h. Using this latter header file, three ANSI C streams are identified as stdin, stdout, and stderr. These correspond in overall operation to cin, cout, and cerr in iostream.h. There are some major differences in the way these streams operate, so this comparison is a rough one offered solely to give the C programmer some conventional points of reference. The major difference lies in the fact that IOSTREAM.H is programmed in an object-oriented manner, whereas stdio.h is not.

Accessing C++ Streams

In C++, the iostream library is very often used instead of the standard I/O library (stdio.h). The reason is that C++ I/O streaming offers a far simpler (i.e., quicker) approach to writing to the standard output and reading from the standard input. All of the definitions and overhead for using I/O streams are contained in the iostream.h header file that is a part of the C++ programming environment. This header file must be **#included** with any program or module that uses C++ I/O streams.

To this point, the content of iostream.h has been discussed only in the most general terms. This may seem frustrating at first, but it is not necessary to know the intimate inner workings of this file. At this point, it is unimportant to know even how C++ classes are used to make true objects. It's only necessary to know that iostream.h is a series of class objects whose personalities allow the programmer to use them for general I/O operations. Again, the important thing about an object (at this juncture) is what it does and not how it does it.

This discussion will concentrate on two of the C++ streams. The first is called cin, which corresponds to stdin, the standard input. The second is cout, the iostream.h equivalent of stdout. With these two streams, a programmer can completely eliminate the standard I/O functions that have always been used for writing to and reading from the console using the standard C programming language. These functions include putchar(), puts(), printf(), scanf(), getc(), getchar(), etc. Such functions are fully supported in C++ and may be used alone or in conjunction with stream access. However, once the true concept of stream access using cin and cout has been grasped, most programmers will simply not want to return to the cumbersome operations involved in using the ANSI C I/O functions.

The cin and cout streams represent an immediate improvement in programming efficiency and are so simple in their operation that they can be learned in a single, short programming session. Most ANSI C programmers soon wonder how they were able to manage without these efficient streaming tools.

I/O Stream Output

The following discussions deal exclusively with writing output to the monitor screen using streaming techniques. This is a logical place to start, since the first code written, compiled, and executed by most practitioners of C was the now-famous "hello, world" program from Kernighan and Ritchie's *The C Programming Language*. The examples that follow can be thought of as the C++ equivalent of this original exercise. It is important for persons learning a new language to begin with routines that write to the screen, because the results of these operations can be immediately visualized as opposed to grasping concepts on a purely abstract basis.

The cout stream is the standard output stream that corresponds to stdout in C stream terminology. It is derived from the ostream class contained in iostream.h. The following program is the old standard presented by the authors of the original C language in the first book ever written on the subject of C programming. This was the first program many beginning C programmers wrote when learning ANSI C.

```
#include <stdio.h>
main()
{

        printf("hello, world\n");

}
```

This program writes the string "hello, world" to the monitor screen, followed by a newline character. The standard input/output (stdio.h) header file is included with this program and contains the definitions necessary to use functions that read data from the keyboard or from files and write data to the monitor or to files. In this case, elements of the printf() function used in this program are defined in stdio.h.

A method of writing the same string to the monitor screen in C++ doesn't require the printf() function, because I/O streaming makes this unnecessary. The following program performs the exact on-screen operations produced by the previous example but in the more straightforward C++ style.

```
#include <iostream.h>
int main()

{

    cout << "hello, world\n";

}
```

It is readily apparent that this program does not directly reference a function at all (other than main(), of course). It uses the cout stream to write to the screen buffer. Stream output is accomplished with a new operator, not available in the ANSI C language. The insertion operator << is also called the *put operator* when used in this type of application.

In ANSI C, several operators share the same keyboard symbol. For example, the multiplicative operator (*) is also the indirection operator, the latter being used in pointer declarations and to return object values from pointers. This is also true in C++, where what is commonly referenced in ANSI C as the left shift operator (<<) serves a multiple purpose as the left shift operator and the insertion operator (as it was used in the program above).

In the following program line, the left operand (cout) is an object of type ostream.

```
            cout << "hello, world\n";
```

This is defined in iostream.h and corresponds to the standard output. The right operand ("hello, world\n") may be of any type for which stream output has been defined, in this case a string. The line above sends the quoted string to the output by means of cout.

Initially, it may appear that sending strings to the monitor in this fashion is very limited, because it does not offer the formatted output capabilities of printf(). However, this is an incorrect assumption, although there are some rare occasions where printf() may be more appropriate. In most instances, this streaming method is considerably easier than using printf() and results in more programming efficiency. The program statement above is far more elegant, and the use of the insertion operator is a welcome improvement to the language.

The following program is written in ANSI C and will later be rewritten in C++ to demonstrate the further capabilities of stream writes.

```
#include <stdio.h>
main()

    int i;

    i = 1097;

    printf("The value in i is %d\n", i);

}
```

This program uses printf() to write a string to the screen, followed by the value in int i. Using this function, it is necessary to supply the %d conversion specification, which tells printf() to convert the value in x to a decimal integer format prior to display.

A C programmer might conclude that writing to cout would be limited only to quoted string expressions when looking at the code presented thus far. The following C++ version of the sample program will prove this to be absolutely untrue.

```
#include <iostream.h>
int main()
{

    int i;

    i = 1097;

    cout << "The value of i is " << i << "\n";

}
```

This program duplicates the screen output of the previous example and displays more advantages of C++ I/O streaming.

Writing to the output stream does not require any conversion specifications, at least not when decimal notation is involved. If the desire is to display the value in a numeric variable in other than decimal notation, a slight modification will be necessary, but even this is far simpler than using the coding formalities of printf().

The following string is the first value written to the output.

```
"The value of i is "
```

The second value is the numeric value in variable i. The variable name is preceded by another insertion (so-called because it inserts data into the stream) operator. The last value written in this particular line is the new-line character (\n), which is enclosed in quotation marks, thus making it a properly terminated string (i.e., \0).

In the above operation, three separate writes to cout have been programmed on the same line. Formatting is accomplished in a direct manner, as opposed to conversion by inserting specifiers into the original string. Overall, this will result in less typing at the keyboard while programming such operations. The following C language program uses printf() in a more complex manner.

```
#include <stdio.h>
main()
{

    int x = 12;
    double y = 469.127;
    char *c = "y multiplied by x = ";

    printf("%s%lf\n", c, y * x);

}
```

This program displays two values using printf(). The first is a string, and the second is a double-precision value based on a mathematical operation. The same thing can be accomplished with the C++ iostream in the following manner.

```
#include <iostream.h>
int main()
{

    int x = 12;
    double y = 469.127;
    char *c = "y multiplied by x = ";

    cout << c << y * x << "\n";

}
```

This method is far simpler and doesn't depend on function calls to accomplish the screen write. A great deal of the simplicity is identified in the lack of conversion specifiers that would be absolutely essential when using printf(). The cout stream doesn't require them at all, and it can handle values of int, short int, long int, float, double, long double, char, char pointer, etc. with equal ease. When displaying values in other than decimal notation, some additional operations are involved. These will be discussed a bit later.

The cout stream defaults to decimal notation in the following formats.

Data Type	Format	Precision
short int	signed and unsigned	decimal integer
int	signed and unsigned	decimal integer
unsigned int	unsigned	decimal integer
long int	signed and unsigned	decimal integer
float	not applicable	six digits
double	not applicable	six digits
long double	not applicable	six digits
char	signed and unsigned	character
char *	not applicable	character string
void *	not applicable	pointer value

The default precision of real (floating point) numbers is six digits with the last digit a rounded value. Both signed and unsigned ints are accommodated with as much ease.

The cout stream offered in C++ is an efficient aid to performing screen writes. It is quite flexible and offers a more expressive means of writing to the standard output, without resorting to function calls and the increased complexities associated with them. Bear in mind that the original C functions such as printf(), which write to the standard output, are still fully supported in C++. However, they probably will not be called on nearly as much as they were in ANSI C (if called at all).

I/O Stream Input

While using cout offers decided advantages in programming many types of applications that write to the screen, the input capabilities offered by iostream.h may be even more appreciated by C programmers who are moving into the C++ programming environment. Using the cin stream, inputting data from the keyboard is greatly expedited when compared with using C language function calls. This is especially true when inputting numeric values from the keyboard. In the area of numeric value retrieval from the keyboard, the intrinsic ANSI C functions have always been terribly sluggish and difficult to use. Additionally, they often create an excellent environment for programmer-induced errors.

Stream input is quite similar to the output operations discussed in the previous section. However, the symbol referred to as the RIGHT shift operator (>>) in ANSI C is used for input. In the C++ streaming environment, this becomes the EXTRACTOR operator. In C++, the multiple use of a single operator is called **overloading**.

The extractor operator is a low-effort (from a code-input standpoint) alternative to the standard input function, scanf(). The latter is the principal function used in the C programming language for the collection of formatted data input of all types from the keyboard. However, the string capture feature of this function is often not utilized, as the standard C function named gets() is called instead for string returns. This enforces an earlier comment about the formatted keyboard retrieval functions in ANSI C being somewhat convoluted and difficult to use, especially in regard to numeric type returns. The gets() function retrieves text and nothing but text, so it has traditionally been used for this purpose even though scanf() might be put to better use in addressing many retrieval tasks. However, the fact is that many programmers (professional and otherwise) dislike scanf() and don't really have a clear understanding of its full capabilities. This is because the format control string specifications are difficult to learn and retain, which is not true of the cin stream in C++.

The cin stream is defined within the istream class and is used in the following format.

```
cin >> x
```

The input from the keyboard is written to variable x in this example. The conversion and formatting functions in such an operation will depend upon the data type of the variable. By default, >> skips whitespace, and then reads in characters appropriate to the type of the input object. As with <<, the >> operator is left-associative and returns its left operand. This allows multiple input operations to be combined into one statement.

The following program is written in ANSI C and retrieves an int value from the keyboard.

```
#include <stdio.h>
main()
{

        int i;

        scanf("%d", &i);

        printf("%d\n", i);

}
```

The scanf() function is used to scan the keyboard for the integer data. The %d conversion specifier informs scanf() about the input data type to be expected within this scan field. The storage source supplied as part of the argument list to scanf() is a pointer to int **i**. Once the data have been retrieved and stored in **i**, they are displayed on the screen by the printf() function.

The C++ iostream equivalent to the preceding program is shown below.

```
#include <iostream.h>
int main()
{

        int i;

        cin >> i;
        cout << i << "\n";

}
```

This program is simpler. It requires less input time when writing the source code, and it better expresses what is actually taking place. The cin stream is the keyboard input. The extractor operator (>>) aims the input at variable i. The keyboard capture is assigned to storage allocated to i, and it is not necessary to supply a pointer, as would be the case with scanf().

In the next line, the value in i and the newline character are aimed at the output (cout) via the insertion operator. From both programming and conceptual standpoints, this method of reading and writing makes a lot more sense. No conversion specifications are necessary, and the two function calls required in the C language versions are done away with.

Both cin and cout allow the conceptualization of targeting. With cin, the input at the keyboard is targeted at the holding variable. In the case of cout, program data are targeted at the monitor. The choice of the operator symbols (<< and >>) reinforces this targeting concept.

Multiple inputs are handled in a logical manner, just as multiple outputs were handled by cout. The following program written in ANSI C begins the discussion of multiple inputs from the keyboard.

```
#include <stdio.h>
main()
{

        char c[40];
        int x, y;

        gets(c);

        scanf("%d%d", &x, &y);

        printf("%c %d %d\n", c, x, y);

}
```

This program declares two int variables and a char array. The gets() function is used to retrieve a string, while scanf() is called to receive the two int values. The collected data are then displayed on the monitor by means of printf().

Using iostream.h, the C++ equivalent is shown below.

```
#include <iostream.h>
int main()
```

```
    {

        char c[40];
        int x, y;

        cin >> c >> x >> y;
        cout << c << " " << x << " " << y << "\n";

    }
```

Variables are declared in exactly the same manner as in the previous
ANSI C program. The keyboard input is targeted first at array c[], and
then at int x, and finally at int y. Like scanf(), any keyboard input that
does not match the variable type being targeted automatically terminates
the scan of a field. Although fields are not being specifically dealt with
in the case of cin, the apparent operation is the same. A carriage return
may be used as a field separator following input of the string, whereas
any key other than one that produces a numeric character will stop the
specific keyboard scan in regard to the integer variables. Like the gets()
function, cin will accept whitespace from the keyboard and incorporate
it into the string. The newline that is received at the end of the string
input is replaced by a null character, as is the case with gets().

Integer Extractors

When cin is used to target data to short ints, ints, unsigned ints, and long
ints, the default action of the extractor is to skip whitespace and convert
to an integer value. This is done by reading input characters until one
is retrieved that is not a legal part of any integer value—this would be
any character other than a numeric type, including, of course, the decimal point, which is not a part of an integer value.

Floating-Point Extractors

When float or double variables are targeted by the extractor operator,
whitespace is skipped and numeric characters are converted to a floating-point value whose default precision is six digits with the last digit
rounded. Again, all input characters are read until one is found that is
not a legal part of a floating-point representation.

I/O Stream Conversions

C++ I/O streaming offers several advantages over alternate means of
reading data from the standard input and writing it to the standard

output. The prospect of using the insertion and extractor operators with cout and cin seems, to most users, to be a more natural approach to read/write operations than functions that accomplish the same thing with greater overhead. However, it is necessary to consider the conversions necessary when numeric quantities are to be displayed or retrieved in other than decimal notation. It is also important to consider the necessity of formatting the display using the insertion operator via the addition of whitespace strings (" "). I/O streaming would be far more attractive if it could have these conversion and formatting features along with the ease of operation that these new operators provide.

Manipulators

An easy method of changing the stream width and other format variables is to use a special function-like operator called a **manipulator**. A manipulator accepts a stream reference as an argument and returns a reference to the same stream. This means that manipulators can be embedded in a chain of insertions or extractions in order to alter the format.

The following program will demonstrate the use of manipulators specifically for numbers conversion.

```
#include <iostream.h>
int main()
{

    int i = 25;
    cout << dec << i << " " << oct << i << " " << hex << i << "\n";

}
```

This program will display the value in **i** (25D) in decimal, octal, and hexadecimal bases. When executed, this program will display the following numbers.

25 31 19

These numbers are the decimal, octal, and hexadecimal values in **i**.

It is already known that the default format is decimal. Therefore, the **dec** manipulator is unnecessary. However, the immediate effect of the **oct** and the **hex** manipulators is apparent. These work in the same manner as the %o and %x conversion specifications that are supplied to the printf() function. Each of these manipulators provides a convenient means of converting a value in one base to the same value in another base.

Some additional aspects to this simple program may be bothersome to some programmers. For instance, it may be annoying to go to the trouble of enclosing in double quotes each whitespace that is to be displayed. The same applies to the newline character that has also been provided as a string argument.

The newline character can be directly addressed by using another manipulator, called **endl**. The previous program could have been written in the following manner.

```
#include <iostream.h>
int main()
{

    int i = 25;

    cout << dec << i << " "  << oct << i << " "   << hex << i << endl;

}
```

The endl manipulator at the end of the expression inserts a newline character and flushes the stream. This takes the place of the more laborious "\n", which has the same number of characters but requires double use of the Shift key.

Regarding the whitespace characters that must be provided as string arguments, there are several methods to address this need more efficiently. Perhaps the most logical (and easiest) method is to call on the **#define** preprocessor directive, as demonstrated by another version of the previous program.

```
#include <iostream.h>
#define space " "
int main()
{

    int i = 25;

    cout << dec << i << space  << oct << i << space << hex << i << endl;

}
```

This results in a very direct and simple method of accomplishing the needed conversions, flushing the buffer and inserting whitespace with a preprocessor definition. The identifier named **space** is #defined as a single-space character (whitespace).

In regard to stream input, the manipulators may be used in a similar manner. The following program accepts input of a hexadecimal value from the keyboard and then displays this value in decimal, octal, and hexadecimal format.

```
#include <iostream.h>
#define space " "
int main()
{

    int i;

    cin >> hex >> i;

    cout << dec << i << space << oct << i << space << hex << i << endl;

}
```

The extractor operator targets the output from cin to variable **i**, with the hex manipulator also targeted in order to set the hexadecimal conversion base format flag. This means that the value input at the keyboard will be a hexadecimal number. This value must be input in pure hex format and without the **0x** specifier used to signify hexadecimal constants incorporated as a part of program source code. Any hex value input via the keyboard will be displayed on the screen in decimal, octal, and hexadecimal formats.

Stream Class Member Functions

The big problem with input in ANSI C involves the handling of whitespace characters where strings are involved. If left purely up to cin and cout in C++, whitespace management still presents a formidable problem in many applications. Fortunately, iostream.h directly addresses the need for such control through stream class member functions that offer a high degree of control when dealing with C++ strings. The stream member functions controlling input include the following.

```
get, getline, ignore, peek, putback, and read
```

Each of these is a member function of the istream class. These member functions are used in a general calling format of

```
cin.<function name>
```

as in

```
cin.get(argument)
```

Using these member functions (methods), any degree of string input format control may be had.

GET()

The **get()** member function is implemented in two different ways. One version is used in the following format.

```
cin.get(char*, num, end)
```

In this usage, char* is a char pointer, and num is an int value that determines the maximum numbers of characters to read based on the formula of num − 1. In this call, **end** is a char value that signals the termination of the read. The following example writes the keyboard input to **array** including all whitespaces.

```
cin.get(array, 25, '\n')
```

It will continue to read keyboard input until 25–1 characters are received or until the newline character ('\n)' is received. Either of these two conditions will halt the keyboard scan. As is the case with the standard gets() function common to ANSI C and C++, the newline character is not read into the array. Rather, it is replaced by the NULL character (\0), resulting in a properly terminated string. This same process will apply to any other type of terminating character used with the IOSTREAM get() function.

The second implementation of **get()** involves the same call, but the argument is a single char variable.

```
char ch;
cin.get(ch);
```

This will read a single character of any type into ch.

It may seem a bit odd to ANSI C programmers that one function (get) can be used for two different purposes. Actually, two different functions that have the same name are involved. This use of the same function name for what are actually two different functions is known as **function overloading**, another advantage offered by C++. Chapter 3 thoroughly deals with this subject, but a simple explanation is in order at this time.

C++ has the ability to differentiate between two or more functions that have been given the same name. This is done by comparing the function argument lists, both of which are supplied in the function prototype or in the function definition if it is made prior to its being called. Since one version of the get() function requires one argument, a char value, and the other requires three, a char pointer, an int, and a char, the C++ compiler will be able to determine which function is actually being called by the differences in their argument parameters. Even if each function only required a single argument, as long as each was of a different type (as determined by the prototype), the distinction between the two could be accurately made. Again, this topic will be more fully discussed in a later chapter, but get used to the idea of functions (and operators) being used to invoke different processes under the same name in C++.

GETLINE()

The **getline()** member function works exactly like the first implementation of get() that was just discussed. It even uses the same argument format.

```
cin.getline(char*, num, end)
```

The only difference in the two lies in the fact that getline() does include the newline character followed by the NULL character. The following input sequence of

```
C++ stream exercise<ENTER>
```

at the keyboard, would result in the array containing the string

```
C++ stream exercise\n\0
```

IGNORE()

The **ignore()** member function is called on to ignore the number of characters specified by its argument. It is used in the following format.

```
cin.ignore(num)
```

Here, **num** is an int value depicting the number of input characters to ignore. When num characters have been input, the remaining characters may be read by a function such as getline() or get(). An example of using the ignore() member function follows.

```
int i = 6;
char array[44];
cin.ignore(i);
cin.get(array, 43, '\n');
```

Assume the keyboard input matches that shown below.

```
Input any string.\n
```

The first six characters of this input are ignored, so the following string is actually placed in array[].

```
any string.\0
```

PEEK()

Not to be confused with peek() functions that are common as special compiler implementations in both C and C++, the **peek()** member function of istream provides the ability to look ahead to the next incoming character from the stream. This function only looks at the next character. It does not actually extract it, therefore it remains in the stream. The following program fragment shows how this function might be used.

```
char c, array[31];

c = cin.peek();
if (c == 'A')
    cin.ignore(1);

cin.get(array, 30, '\n');
```

Here, peek() simply reads the first character in the istream buffer. The value of this character is assigned to char c. However, the character has not been extracted from the stream. It has only been identified as the next character that can be extracted. Next, an if-statement is used to test for the 'A' character in char c. If present, then ignore() is called in order to keep this character from being written to array[] by the get() function that follows. The peek() function is used to test for the first character in the input being the 'A'. Often, this function is used (in conjunction with other code) to make a filter when building an array of characters one character at a time. Each character would be filtered through the peek() construct before it is written to an array. Any triggering characters could be removed by using the if-statement conditional test above in conjunction with ignore().

PUTBACK()

The **putback()** member function is similar in operation to the standard C/C++ ungetc() function or macro equivalent. It is used to put an extracted character back into streambuf, and is used in the following format.

```
cin.putback(c)
```

Variable **c** is the last character that has been extracted from the stream. The following program fragment shows how this could be used.

```
char c, first_array[55], second_array[30];

cin >> c;
if (isupper(c)) {
    cin.putback(c);
    cin.get(first_array, 54, '\n');
}
```

```
        else {
            cin.putback(c);
            cin.get(second_array, 29, '\n');
        }
```

The purpose of this code group is to write any keyboard input that begins with an uppercase character (ASCII 65-90) into first_array[]. Any input that does not begin with an uppercase letter will be written to second_array[]. The cin stream writes the first character input to char c, its value having been tested in the if-statement construct. If it is an uppercase letter, then putback() pushes it back on the stream buffer, and the subsequent call to get() causes the entire stream contents to be written to first_array[]. If the conditional test is negative, then putback() is used again and the entire streambuf contents are read into second_array[].

READ()

The **read()** member function is similar in usage to get(), but it recognizes no terminating character. This function reads a specified number of characters into the array that serves as its first argument. It is called in the following format.

```
            cin.read(array, num)
```

Variable **num** is the number of characters to be read. (Note: This is different from get(), which reads in num – 1 characters.) Any type of character (standard, whitespace, binary, etc.) may be read into the array argument.

While all of these member functions have been discussed and demonstrated within a framework of the standard input, they are even more valuable when applied to file streams, which are discussed later in this chapter.

Output Stream Class Member Functions

The iostream header file is a combination of classes of which ostream is the standard output. This class also offers two member functions that may be called when cout is not the best choice for performing a specific job with the precision sought by the programmer. The two member functions are put() and write() and should not be confused with any standard

C or C++ functions that may have the same name. These are ostream member functions that can be used only as a part of the ostream class. They are made available when iostream.h is #included with any program that intends to use them. These functions are called in the following formats.

```
cout.put(char)
cout.write(char *, num)
```

This format uses the member-of operator for invocation. The put() function is used to insert all character types into the stream buffer (streambuf). This includes normal, binary, and whitespace characters. The write() member function writes a string of **num** characters into the stream buffer.

In all cases, the member functions may be used to access the standard I/O streams. However, they are far more useful when used with file streams.

Format Control

The stream operations discussed to this point do many of the things that have traditionally been accomplished in the past with stdio.h and the ANSI C functions that read and write to the streams defined in this header file. However, functions such as printf() and scanf() offer many format control features. These same features can be obtained when using C++ stream conventions under iostream.h.

As was stated earlier, **ios** is the base class from which all other stream classes are derived. The ios class contains six format-control member functions.

```
fill()         -- returns the fill character value
fill(num)      -- changes the fill character value to num
precision()    -- returns the current precision value
precision(num) -- changes precision to num places
width()        -- returns the current field width
width(num)     -- changes the current field width
```

The following C++ program demonstrates the use of the fill(num) and width(num) member functions.

```
#include <iostream.h>
int main()
{
    int i;

    cout.fill('.');

    for (i = 1; i <= 9; ++i) {
        cout.width(i);
        cout << i << endl;
    }
}
```

When executed, this program will produce the following display.

```
1
.2
..3
...4
....5
.....6
......7
.......8
........9
```

This program displays a sequential series of numbers (1–9) in an ever-increasing field width of 1 through 9 places. The '.' character has been specified as the fill character. The default fill character is the space (whitespace). The width member function does not permanently change the default field width, which is 0. When called, this function changes the field for the next write. Afterward, the field width returns to its default unless width() is executed again and prior to the next write. However, the fill(num) member function resets the default to the argument value.

This new fill character will be used to pad all fields until changed by another call to fill(num).

The following program uses the precision(num) member function.

```cpp
#include <iostream.h>
int main()
{
    double d = 44.127645 / 13.22687;
    int i;

    for (i = 1; i <= 10; ++i) {
        cout.precision(i);
        cout << d << endl;
    }
}
```

When executed, this program will produce the following screen display.

```
3.3
3.34
3.336
3.3362
3.33622
3.336216
3.336216
3.33621598
3.336215976
3.3362159755
```

It can be seen that the precision of numbers displayed in the cout stream has been changed by the precision(num) member function. This function changes the default precision value of 6 to whatever int argument is supplied. This alteration of precision will remain in effect until specifically changed within the program.

To detect the current precision, width, or fill, the alternate member functions are called in the following format.

```cpp
i = cout.width();
i = cout.fill();
i = cout.precision();
```

The value returned in **i** specifies the current state.

The member functions have been shown in connection with the cout stream, but they can be used, judiciously, with the cin stream as well in order to set the width, precision, and fill characters of the input stream.

The iomanip.h file contains a number of member functions called **parameterized manipulators**. These work in a manner similar to those just described, but may be inserted directly as arguments in C++ streams.

The following table shows a listing of these manipulators.

```
setbase(int num)        --    sets the conversion base
                              (8 == octal; 10 == decimal; 16 == hexadecimal)
setfill(int num)        --    sets fill character to int
setprecision(int num)   --    sets real numbers precision to (num) places
setw(int num)           --    sets filed width to int characters
```

These compare with the simple manipulators discussed previously as follows.

```
setbase(num)    --   DEC, OCT, HEX
setfill(num)    --   fill(num)
setprecision    --   precision(num)
setw(num)       --   width(num)
```

These can be used in the following manner.

```
#include <iostream.h>
#include <iomanip.h>
void main(void)
{

    double a = 4.67512981351;
    double b = 2.19183245616;

    cout << setprecision(4) << a << "\n" << setprecision(8) << b << endl;

}
```

This will result in the following display.

```
4.6751
2.19183245
```

Notice that the iomanip.h header file is #included with the program along with iostream.h. This usage of the precision manipulator allows the precision to be changed within a single source code line. Using the simple manipulator, precision(num), this same exercise would necessarily be written as follows.

```
#include <iostream.h>
int main()
{

    double a = 4.67512981351;
    double b = 2.19183245616;

    cout.precision(4);
    cout << a << endl;
    cout.precision(8);
    cout << b << endl;

}
```

Obviously, the former example makes better sense. The other parameterized manipulators may be used in a like fashion to determine field width, fill characters, and numeric base.

C++ File Streams

The C programming language certainly presents programmers with an unusual syntax, but its I/O functions, whether for file access, console access, or even string access, treat I/O in a highly generic fashion. For instance, printf(), the standard output formatted write function, is matched by fprintf(), the function used for writing formatted output to a disk file. In fact, printf() actually calls fprintf() with the stdout file argument resulting in a write to the standard output. These two functions operate in the same manner, so the transition to file writes is quite simple once the programmer knows how to write to the monitor.

In C++, the same may be said of streams, stream member functions, stream operators, and manipulators. The previous discussions have dealt with writing and reading information from the console (stdin/stdout). The same principles can be applied to simple file I/O without resorting to the standard filekeeping functions found in stdio.h.

FSTREAM.H

The header file **fstream.h** defines the C++ stream classes that support file input and output. The classes defined in this header file inherit the insertion and extraction operations from iostream.h. The fstream.h header file provides constructors and member functions for creating and handling simple file I/O. In many instances, these operations can completely take the place of the more conventional file I/O manipulations commonly used in ANSI C. These latter functions are fully available in C++ as well, but in most cases, they will not be necessary or desirable due to the convenience extras C++ offers.

Two classes contained in fstream.h are **ifstream** and **ofstream**. These correspond to the istream and ostream classes in iostream.h. They handle, respectively, file input and file output as do their counterparts for standard I/O. The member functions available in iostream.h, which were discussed earlier in this chapter, are carried over into fstream.h. It is within this environment that these member extraction/insertion functions realize their full potential.

The following program is written in ANSI C. It opens a disk file for read operations and another file for write operations. The contents of the first file are then copied sequentially, one character at a time, into the second.

```c
#include <stdio.h>
main()
{

    FILE *fp *ffp;
    int i;

    if ((fp = fopen("file_one", "r")) == NULL) {
        printf("File Open Error\n");
        exit(0);
    }

    if ((fp = fopen("file_two", "r")) == NULL) {
        printf("File Open Error\n");
        exit(0);

    }

    while ((i = fgetc(fp)) != EOF)
```

```
        fputc(i, ffp);

    fclose(fp);
    fclose(ffp);

}
```

Although this program accomplishes a very simple task, it consumes a sizable amount of overhead due to the necessity of checking for error returns. Using the fgetc() function, data are extracted from file_one, one character at a time, and then written in the same manner to file_two. When the end-of-file (EOF) is returned, fclose() is called to close the two files.

There is a simpler way of accomplishing the same task using the enhanced streaming conventions available in C++. The following program #includes the fstream.h header file to gain access to files in a manner similar to accessing the standard I/O.

```
#include <fstream.h>
int main()
{

    char ch;

    ifstream fp("file_one");  // open file_one
    if (!fp) {                // test for bad open
        cerr << "File Open Error" << endl;
        exit(0);
    }

    ofstream ffp("file_two"); // open file_two
    if (!ffp) {               // test for bad open
        cerr << "File Open Error" << endl;
        exit(0);
    }

    while (ffp && fp.get(ch))   // read file_one data
        ffp.put(ch);            // write file_two data

}
```

This C++ program performs exactly the same operations as did the standard C program. Through the definitions in fstream.h, ifstream is used to open a file for input. The file name, **file_one**, is a string argument that is tied to fp, the file handle. The following line is a conditional test for the successful opening of the file whose handle is fp.

```
if (!fp)
```

This same method may be used in ANSI C for checking the successful opening of files. In the above example, however, the ! symbol is an operator function that is a member of the ios class. Just as function names can be overloaded in C++, the same applies to operators. This is an example of *operator overloading* and will be discussed in more detail in Chapter 3.

This construct returns a non-zero integer when an error has occurred and a zero value when no error state exists. Using this stream operator function allows for the detection of errors during stream I/O, and once a stream is placed in an error state, all attempts to read or write information from or to the stream will be ignored until the error condition is corrected.

In discussing this program, one must assume that file_one already exists and that its contents are to be read into file_two, which is yet to be created. The creation process takes place within ostream. This opens file_two and gives it a handle named ffp. Next, a **while** loop that tests both file handles for a return value of zero is incorporated. Such a return value indicates an error condition, usually brought on by an end-of-file (EOF) return. Within the **while** clause, the following expression is found.

```
fp.get(c)
```

This uses the get() member function to get the character from fp into char c. At the same time, the error condition of both file streams (fp && ffp) is being tested. Within the loop body, the expression puts the character found in char c into the second file.

```
ffp.put(c);
```

When all data have been read from the first file, an EOF condition will be returned to **while** and the program will terminate.

The fstream.h header file is the file stream equivalent to iostream.h. Stream classes ifstream and ofstream compare to istream and ostream in the latter header file, while filebuf is the file stream equivalent of streambuf. Another class contained in fstream.h is fstreambase, a file stream equivalent of ios, the base class in iostream.h.

Open()

The above file-handling examples show a very simple form of file stream I/O. For simple file operations these methods are fine, but for more intensive file access, it will be necessary to use the fstream member function named **open()**. This function accepts as its arguments the name of the file to be opened followed by the mode in which the opening is to occur. Here, one of several mode enumerators garnered from the ios class can be used.

```
app       --    open for append
ate       --    open file and seek to end of file
binary  --      open file in binary mode
in        --    open for input
nocreate -- erases file if it exists or does nothing if file does not exist
noreplace --    does nothing if file exists
out       --    open for output
trunc   --      open file (if it doesn't exist) or if it exists, erase file contents.
```

The ANSI C programmer will probably notice immediately that **in**, **out**, and **app** closely compare with the fopen() file modes of **w**, **r**, and **a**.

These enumerators are a part of the ios class from which the classes in fstream.h are derived. To use these enumerators within the open() member function, it is necessary to use the scope resolution operator (::). This operator is fully explained in the next chapter, but for now, think of it as the complete path to the **in** (in this case) enumerator that is contained in the ios class. The expression **ios::in** invokes the **in** enumerator in the ios class. A comparison may be made with this expression and a DOS **full** filename such as **\count\run.exe** where the file named **run.exe** is contained in a directory named **count**.

The open() member function can accept three arguments. In addition to the name and open mode of the file, the third argument is the file mask, which defaults to **ios::openprot**. This is the standard file mask, and since it is the default for all uses of open(), it is not necessary to include it specifically as an argument.

The following program accomplishes the same thing as the previous example, but it uses the open() member function.

```cpp
#include <fstream.h>
#include <stdlib.h>
int main()
{

    char c;
    fstream fp, ffp;

    fp.open("file_one", ios::in);   // open file_one

    if (!fp) {   // test for bad open
        cerr << "File Stream Error on Opening file_one." << endl;
        exit(0);

    }
    ffp.open("file_two", ios::out); // open file_two

    if (!ffp) { // test for bad open
        cerr << "File Stream Error on Opening file_two." << endl;
        exit(0);
    }

    while (ffp && fp.get(c))     // read file_one data
        ffp.put(c);              // write file_two data

    fp.close();
    ffp.close();


}
```

The open() member function contains only two arguments, which means that the default file mask argument is being used. Other than the manner in which the files are opened, this program is very similar to the previous example.

File Stream Positioning

The fstream.h header file contains the classes, member functions, enumerators, and so on to handle all file I/O operations, although many of these tools have been inherited from the classes in iostream.h. File positioning member functions are also available, and these closely parallel ANSI C counterparts.

Throughout this text, constant references are made to ANSI C, the language the reader currently knows best. It should be readily apparent that these references are not forced in any way. For the most part, C++ enhancements draw naturally on many of the conventions that have been an integral part of ANSI C. It is only necessary to make the appropriate mental connections to move smoothly into a full C++ programming environment.

C++ file streams offer seekg(), seekp(), tellg(), and tellp(), which can be compared with fseek() and ftell() in ANSI C. The seekg() and tellg() member functions seek and report get or read positions, while seekp() and tellp() seek and report the put or write positions. The tell functions require no argument, as they simply report the current file position.

```
g_position = file_one.tellg();
```

This example returns to **g_position** the current get position of the file.

```
p_position = file_one.tellp();
```

This one returns the current put position of the file name file_one.

The seek functions accept two arguments, the first being the number of bytes that is to be offset from the reference, and the second is the reference, which can be one of three enumerators defined in the ios class.

```
beg    --    seek from beginning of file
cur    --    seek from current file position
end    --    seek from end of file
```

Assuming that file_one is opened for get operations, the following lines are applicable.

```
file_one.seekg(57, ios::beg); // seek 57 bytes from file beginning
file_one.seekg(57, ios::cur); // seek 57 bytes from current position
file_one.seekg(57, ios::end); // seek 57 bytes from file end
```

If the file has been opened for output (i.e., ios::out), then the seekp()
member function would be called to seek out a new put position.

Summary

Many C programmers who are making the transition to C++ take great
delight in discovering the advantages of I/O streaming in the latter language. The techniques involved are direct and easy. One must remember that C++ was developed by professional programmers who have had
the advantage of working with ANSI C for many years. C++, then, contains many of the features ANSI C lacked. C++ I/O streams are not too
good to be true; they are language features that were what the original
language needed to be more useful.

   With C++ I/O streams, the input and output of data are conducted in
a more logical and direct manner. ANSI C was always a bit weak in the
I/O area, at least when compared with other features of this original language. Through streaming techniques, the programmer does not need to
build a lot of extraneous safety or conversion features into a program. The
addressing of I/O operations is now in tune with the compact and expressive nature of the rest of the language.

Chapter 3

++++++++++++++

Procedural-Based C++

C++ is a superset of the ANSI C programming language, one that allows for object-oriented operations to be easily carried out. OOP requires a complete rethinking of how things are accomplished when one is accustomed to working with a procedural-based programming language. For this reason, many object-oriented programs will appear foreign to the ANSI C programmer. The programming philosophy is radically different, and there are numerous additions to the syntax of C++.

However, most ANSI C programmers begin learning C++ in a procedural-based manner, the manner that is most familiar to those coming from an ANSI C environment. ANSI C is accurately rated as a procedural-based or non-object-oriented language. C++ offers object-oriented capabilities, but the latter do not have to be immediately embraced. The learning process entails a gradual transition toward the additional features offered by C++, one of which is OOP.

Of immediate interest to the C programmer is the fact that C++ offers many additions and extensions that allow it to be used as a very powerful form of C language, addressing tasks in a procedural-based manner. Through such operations, C++ is used exactly like C in programming philosophy. However, the additional tools offered by C++ make for an even more powerful procedural-based approach.

This chapter will explore some of the additions offered by C++ that can be immediately grasped by the C programmer without having to completely change his or her programming philosophy. It will take more time to embrace the total concept of OOP, but prior to adopting an object-oriented concept, C++ may be efficiently used to excellent advantage through these additions alone.

Declarations

Using ANSI C, all variable and function declarations must be made at the beginning of the program or function. If additional declarations are needed, the programmer must return to the declaration block(s) in order to make the necessary adjustments or insertions. Again, all declarations must be made before any statements are executed.

C++ does not operate with this restriction. Variables may be declared anywhere in a program (prior to their being used). This allows the programmer to declare many variables in closer proximity to the program statements in which they are used if this approach is desired. The following program demonstrates this feature.

```
#include <stdio.h>
int main()
{

    int i;

    for (i = 0; i < 75; ++i)
        printf("%d\n", i);

    double j;

    for (j = 1.79154; j < 22.58131; j += .001)
        printf("%lf\n", y);

}
```

This program would be strictly illegal in ANSI C, but C++ has the capability of making declarations at any point in a program or function. The following program is a rewrite of this one, showing how declarations may be made legally at any point in the program.

```
#include <iostream.h>
int main()
{


    for (int i = 0; i < 99; ++i)
        cout << i << endl;

    for (double j = 1.79154; j < 22.58131; j += .0001)
        cout << j << endl;


}
```

Here, the declarations of the two variables are made within the **for** loop structures. This may be an even more expressive way of declaring variables for certain programming applications, which is especially true if a variable is to be used for one, short-lived purpose and then discarded.

Placing declared variables closer to the point in the logical execution chain where they are to be used greatly helps the programmer to keep track of variable names. The last program was a simple example of this, but if several thousand lines of code were added to separate the two loops, the value of this asset becomes far more apparent. This is not to say that declarations should be scattered arbitrarily throughout a program. However, in many situations, for the sake of clarity, it is more appropriate to make declarations closer to their point of usage.

Comment Lines

C++ supports two types of comments. Standard comment lines such as the one shown below are supported just as they are in ANSI C.

```
/* ANSI C Comment Line */
```

The compiler will ignore everything that follows the /* delimiter. These comments are meant to aid persons reading the source code. The ignore procedure is terminated when the */ delimiter is encountered.

C++ offers another type of comment delimiter that is a little easier to use, but it can be applied only to comments that can be contained on a single line. The following line demonstrates the C++ // comment delimiter.

```
// C++ comment line
```

The compiler ignores any line or portion of a line that starts with the // delimiter and terminates the ignore procedure at the end of the line. There is no programmer-supplied terminating delimiter.

Both types of comments are legal and should be utilized by C++ programmers. The /* */ version is used for comments that exceed one line in length. The // delimiter is used for one-line comments only.

Casts

In ANSI C, the **cast** operator is used to coerce data of one type to another type. Therefore, if variable **i** is an integer and **l_change()** is a function that requires a long int data type, then the following statement coerces the value in **i** to type long int.

```
l_change((long) i);
```

Under C++, a new type of cast syntax may be used. This is shown below.

```
l_change(long(i))
```

In this usage, the cast type name is not enclosed in parentheses, but its object is. This form of casting looks like a function call, and many programmers feel it is more expressive. C++ offers two methods of accomplishing the same cast operations, and either or both may be used in the same program. Both forms accomplish exactly the same thing. It is up to the programmer to choose the method that provides the desired expression in the source code.

Enum

Enumerated data types are fully supported in C++, but they are treated in a slightly different manner than those in ANSI C. In C++, the contents of an enumerated list are of type **unsigned char** or **int**, depending on the values involved. If all values can be represented as unsigned chars, then this is the type of each enumerator. If not, they are of type **int**. In other words, unsigned char is the standard default value unless the values are beyond the range of this data type. In such instances, the type is changed to **int**. However, when an enumerator is used in an expression, its value is always converted to an int.

In C++, the **enum** tag name is classified as a type name. While ANSI C considers all enums to be of type int, a C++ enumerated value is its own separate type. This means that C++ does not allow for an int value to be automatically converted to an enum value. However, an enumerated value can be used in place of an int. The following code segment will explain further.

```
enum color { Red, Blue, Green, Amber };

int x = Green; // Used in place of an integer
color sscreen = Red;
color background = 148; // ERROR!!!
```

This construct would be perfectly legal in ANSI C, but it generates an error message when compiled in a C++ environment. This occurs because **color** is now (in C++) a type name, and the numeric constant, 16, is an int data type. The way to make this work in C++ is to cast the numeric constant to the proper type.

```
color background = (color) 148;
```

This will correct the problem because the value assigned to **color background** has been cast to type **color**.

In discussing casts, it was noted earlier that C++ will support the standard method of casting used in ANSI C, but an alternate method is offered.

```
color background = color(148);
```

Some programmers prefer this method of casting. Others may find it confusing because the above construct might look more like a call to a function named color().

Returning to the subject of enum implementation under C++, we discover another marked difference. The C++ environment supports the creation of anonymous enums (i.e., enums without tags). Such an entity is declared by simply leaving out the tag name. The following code segment is an example of an anonymous enum declaration.

```
enum { Red, Green, Blue, Amber };
```

Used in this manner, the enum constants may be referenced in the same manner as regular constants as is shown below.

```
int sscreen = Red;
int border = Green;
```

One hopes that there will be little confusion about this type of usage. Later discussions will deal with other anonymous C++ entities.

Const

In both C and C++, any value declared as constant may not be modified by the program in any way. While ANSI C does offer **const** values, it doesn't implement them in the same manner as C++. In the latter environment, const values can be used with far more flexibility. First of all, in C++, const values can take the place of any literal constant, allowing the user to create typed constants instead of having to resort to #define to create constants that have no type information.

In ANSI C, const values are global in scope. They are visible outside of the function in which they are declared unless they are also declared static. In C++, all const values are **static** by default and thus must be considered local.

Structs and Unions

In C++, structs and unions are often referred to as *enhanced,* since they can contain both data definitions and functions. However, two changes have been made in C++ that may affect existing C programs. Struct and union tags are considered to be type names, just as if they had been declared by the **typedef** keyword. The following code fragment demonstrates an ANSI C method of struct usage.

```
struct frame {
    int i;
    float f;

};

struct frame iname;
```

This declares a struct with the tag name **frame** and then creates an instance named **iname**.

In C++, things are much simpler, as shown by the following example.

```
struct frame {
    int i;
    float f;
};

frame iname;
```

These same conventions apply to unions. To maintain compatibility with ANSI C, C++ will accept the older syntax, but as C++ continues to evolve toward some sort of accepted standard, such compatibilities may be deleted from the language.

Other Differences

The following discussions cover some operations that will be familiar to ANSI C programmers. However, C++ responds to them in a slightly different manner. Fortunately, the adjustments needed to adapt these operations to this new environment are quite logical. The ANSI C programmer should have little difficulty in responding appropriately to these differences. Again, many of these examples fall into the category of "features that ANSI C should have had but didn't."

Void Pointers

The **void** data type represents a null value. This type is incorporated into ANSI C, although it was not supported by the original C programming language. Functions that do not produce a useful (or needed) return should be declared data type void. In C++, it is more appropriate to think of a void pointer as a pointer to any data type.

In the original C programming language, pointers of type char were the generic types because of their 1-byte alignment. Functions such as malloc() and calloc() in this earlier language typically returned pointers of type char. In C++, the void pointer type has the same address alignment as a char pointer (1-byte). Therefore, void pointers are now normally used in place of the earlier and less expressive char pointer types (where applicable).

Void can be used to define pointers to generic items. Such pointers might be passed to functions that are not allowed to make assumptions about the type of object they access. Prior to the introduction of void, a pointer of type char might have been used to reference some part of memory without having to be concerned with the type of data stored there. The original (pre-ANSI C) version of malloc(), the memory allocation function, returned a char pointer. Under ANSI C and C++, malloc returns a pointer of type void.

In C++, the main idea behind a void pointer is that of a type that can be used conveniently to access any type of object, because it is, more or less, type-independent. This avoids much of the typecasting that would be required if the pointer were of another type, such as char. However, there is a significant difference in how C++ and ANSI C handle the assignment of void pointers to other pointer types. For example, the simple program that follows works in ANSI C but not in C++.

```
int main()
{

    void *vptr
    int *iptr

    vptr = iptr
    iptr = vptr           // Incorrect in C++

}
```

This is fine in ANSI C, but C++ would view the second assignment as a type mismatch, and an error message would be generated by the compiler. A pointer of type void can be assigned any type, but the reverse is not true unless the cast operator is used to coerce the void pointer to the appropriate type (char * in the above example). In C++, the last line of the code fragment should read as follows.

```
                    iptr = (int*) vptr;
```

In a C++ environment, any type of pointer may be assigned to a void pointer without casting.

Main()

The intrinsic main() function in C++ is prototyped in the same manner as all functions used within this environment. Under the AT&T standard for C++, main() may take one of two forms.

```
intmain ()
int main (int argc, char *argv[])
```

The former is used when the program is invoked without arguments. Using the second form, command line options are permitted. The *argv* parameter is an int value that names the total number of arguments, while the second parameter is an array of pointers to the actual arguments.

While these two forms are the only ones acceptable under the AT&T standard for C++, many C++ compilers will allow other forms. For instance, the Borland C++ compiler is not at all particular. As a matter of fact, the company documentation for this compiler uses main() in the following format.

```
int main(void)
```

This works in a normal fashion with this particular compiler, as will the following forms.

```
main()
void main(void)
void main()
```

However, there is no guarantee that these forms will continue to be supported. To be on the safe side, all C++ programs should adhere to the standard. Therefore, all program examples in this text not requiring command line arguments will define this function as *int main()*.

Char Constants

In C, most compilers store single char constants as ints unless a char constant is part of a string. In such a case, it is stored as a char. This means that in C, the following expression would be true.

```
sizeof('a') == sizeof(int)
```

However, this is not true in C++, where the single char constant is treated as a single byte and is not intrinsically converted to the size of an int. In C++, the following expression would be TRUE.

```
sizeof('a') == 1;
```

In C++, a single character constant is of type char (1 byte). Multicharacter constants in both C and C++ are of type int. When writing code in C++, the user must be aware of the differences in the conventions of this language and those that apply under ANSI C.

New Features in C++

C++ offers a multitude of new features that are designed to enhance OOP. However, many of these may be immediately utilized in a procedural-based manner that will help transitioning ANSI C programmers. When dealing with the subject of object-oriented programming, always remember that most of the OOP extras that have been made a part of C++ are not limited solely to OOP operations. They have valuable uses in procedural-based programming as well.

ASM

A new feature of C++ is the **asm** keyword that allows direct insertion of assembly language code within the C++ program. Some C compilers have offered this capability in the past, but it has never been an official part of the language (i.e. part of the ANSI standard). With the coming of C++, the **asm** keyword now becomes a standard language feature.

Each assembly language statement must be preceded by this keyword, which means that each **asm** statement becomes a C++ statement. This new keyword may be used in several different formats, including the following.

```
asm statement;

asm { statement
      statement
      statement
}

asm {statement; statement; statement;}

asm statement; statement

asm statement
```

To the seasoned ANSI C programmer, this is a bit confusing at first glance, because the assembly language statements that follow the asm keyword are not dependent on the semicolon ';' terminator in all cases. The newline character at the end of an assembly language instruction is sufficient termination. For asm statements, the newline takes the place of the more conventional ';'.

This means that

```
asm mov y, 3
```

is just as valid as

```
asm mov y, 3;
```

When grouping a number of asm statements, the semicolon is necessary only if they all appear on the same line (no newline).

```
asm {pop ax; pop ds; iret;}
```

This can also be written without the semicolons in the following format.

```
asm {
     pop ax
     pop ds
     iret
}
```

Whenever the asm keyword is encountered, the assembly language code controlled by this keyword is compiled with the C++ program as a C++ statement(s). This makes it very convenient to insert assembly language routines anywhere within the C++ source code.

New and Delete

In ANSI C, dynamic memory allocation/deallocation is accomplished through the use of the UNIX library functions, such as malloc() and free() or through specialized functions that are relevant to one type of compiler only and, thus, not portable. The malloc() function sets aside blocks of memory, while free() is used to release these allocated blocks. C++ defines a new method of performing dynamic memory allocation using the **new** and **delete** operators.

The following example illustrates the ANSI C method of memory allocation.

```
main()
{
    int *i;

    i = (int *) malloc(sizeof(int));
    *i = 32023;

    printf("%d\n", *i);

    free(i);

}
```

In C++, the new operator can be used to replace completely the standard C function malloc(). The delete operator takes the place of free(). Using C++ conventions, the previous program could be written in the following manner.

```
#include <iostream.h>
int main()
{

    int *i;

    i = new int;   // return pointer to int-size block
    *i = 32023;    // assign value

    cout << *i;    // display value

    delete i;      // free allocated memory

}
```

The C++ method of using the new and delete operators is a simpler and far more direct approach to allocating and freeing up memory for the pointer.

A constant value cannot be used directly with the **new** operator. The example below is an attempt to do just this.

```
                    i = new 384;    //Incorrect
```

The obvious intent here is to set aside 384 bytes of data referenced by the pointer **i**. Although it is easy to accomplish this with the **new** operator, the above example is incorrect and is shown because it represents some of the (flawed) attempts made by ANSI C programmers who are making the transition to C++.

   The following ANSI C program introduces a discussion that should help to clarify this matter.

```c
/* ANSI C Version */
#include <stdio.h>
main()
{

    char *i;

    i = (char *) malloc(384);

    gets(i);

    puts(i);

    free(i);

}
```

To accomplish the same thing in C++ using the new and delete operators, the following program could be used.

```cpp
// C++ Version
#include <iostream.h>
int main()
{

    char *i;

    i = new char[384]; //allocate block of 384 chars

    cin >> i;
    cout << i << "\n";

    delete i;
```

This method of memory allocation is a vast improvement over that used in ANSI C. Note that pointer **i** is assigned a value of

```
new char[384]
```

which means that the total memory allocation will be

```
384 X char
```

or 384 times the number of bytes allocated to a char data type. In most implementations, a total of 384 bytes will be allocated.

In contrast, if the assignment line had been written as

```
i = new int[384]
```

then a total of 768 bytes (384 × 2) would be allocated, assuming that 2 bytes are allocated to an int data type. This format provides a definite programming advantage in that the sizeof() operator is not necessary to allocate the correct amount of storage. Portability is still maintained across different systems/compilers.

If **new** cannot allocate the requested amount of memory, its return value is NULL. This copies the operation of a malloc() call, which also returns NULL when an allocation error occurs. The above examples are as simple as possible and do not include checks for the NULL return. However, good programming practice absolutely requires such checks to avoid memory overwrites. A simple check can be made using an if-statement construct, as shown below.

```
if ((i = new char[384]) == NULL)
     exit(0);
```

Since the new and delete operators can take the place of malloc() and its memory release function in the standard function set, and because these operators offer a simpler and more direct approach, it makes sense to use them exclusively.

From the standpoint of memory allocation, it is necessary to use either the ANSI C/UNIX functions (malloc, free, etc.) or the new and delete

C++ operators. Trying to mix and match both types of dynamic management systems can lead to serious allocation problems and general inconsistencies.

The **new** operator will always return a pointer of the correct type without this type being specified by the programmer, as the example below illustrates.

```
int *i;

i = new[45];
```

In this code fragment, **new** will return a pointer of type int, because the operand (i) is an int type. It is unnecessary to cast the pointer to the correct type as would be the case with malloc() or calloc(). This is one of the major advantages of a memory allocation operator as opposed to a function that performs a similar operation.

The new and delete operators may be used to create (and destroy) multidimensional arrays as shown below.

```
int *i;

i = new int[4][50];   //create array
// array is put to use

delete i;   // destroy array
```

Here, an array of 50 ints (two-dimensional) is created, setting aside a total of 400 bytes (assuming 2-byte integers). There are some restrictions on this usage, in that the first dimension in the array may be any valid expression, but the remaining dimension(s) must always be an int constant. For example, the following expression is perfectly valid.

```
i = 4;
x = new int[i][50];
```

However, the next one is strictly illegal.

```
i = 4;
x = new int[2][i];
```

Every array dimension but the first one must be expressed as int constants. In every case, the **new** operator returns a pointer to the first element in the array. This operator does *not* automatically initialize any memory objects it creates. The contents of a memory block allocated by **new** using the methods discussed to this point are meaningless until initialized within the program.

The new and delete operators serve a very useful purpose in taking the place of the standard library functions for allocation and freeing of memory blocks. However, these operators were especially designed for an object-oriented environment where objects must be created and later destroyed. When new is used to allocate memory for any object other than an array, an optional initializer may be incorporated as shown below.

```
char *c;
int *x;
double *d;

c = new char('B');
x = new int(0);
d = new double(3.14159);
```

In this code fragment, three pointers are declared of type char, int, and double, respectively. When the **new** operator is invoked to allocate storage for each of these, the optional initializer is used, which initializes the blocks to the values specified. The initializer values are contained in parentheses and must match or have the capability of being cast to the type specified. For instance, if the initializer value for the double pointer was specified as 3, this would be cast to 3.0000000, while an initializer value to the int pointer of 22.19372 would be cast to the int value of 22. If the initializer values cannot be converted to the proper type, then initialization does not take place and the object is garbage.

Objects created by the new operator exist until they are destroyed by the delete operator or until the program ends. The delete operator is the only means of freeing up memory allocated by the new operator while execution is taking place. Failing to free up memory that has been allocated by **new** and is no longer needed is a poor programming practice that may result in insufficient memory for other applications.

Even though program termination will automatically free up all memory allocated by new, it is still essential to always delete any allocated memory before the program ends. The free() function will have no effect on releasing these blocks. Conversely, memory allocated by malloc() cannot be released by the delete operator.

It is important to understand that the delete operator can be used for purposes other than freeing memory allocated by new. For instance, delete can be called to erase the address in a pointer without deleting the pointer variable, proper. The following program shows a simple example of accomplishing this.

```
#include <iostream.h>
int main()
{

    char *a, *b;

    b = "Language";
    a = b;

    cout << a << endl;

    delete a;

    cout << a << endl;

}
```

In this example, pointer **b** is assigned the address of the string constant, "Language". Next, pointer **a** is assigned the address in pointer **b**. Now, both pointers contain the address of the first byte in "Language". Using cout, the object referenced by pointer **a** ("Language") is displayed on the screen. Next, the delete operator is used to destroy the address in pointer **a**. The next line displays the object referenced by **a** again, but this will result in garbage being written to the screen, because the address in pointer **a** has been destroyed.

One decided advantage of using new and delete for memory allocation/destruction is slightly faster execution time, since built-in (intrinsic) operators are used as opposed to functions. However, compilation times for programs using new and delete will be slightly longer than when using the standard library memory functions. This is a fair trade-off, as execution time should be of paramount importance.

Anonymous Unions

Earlier in this chapter, the subject of anonymous enums was discussed. C++ also offers anonymous unions. Simply put, an anonymous union declares a set of members that share the same memory address. This certainly meets the definition of a standard union in ANSI C. However, an anonymous union does not have a tag name. This means that the union elements may be accessed directly. This can result in great savings in source code input time when writing programs that rely heavily on unions.

The following example is written in ANSI C and uses a standard union.

```
union test {
    int x;
    float y;
    double z;
};

main()
{

    union test access;

    access.x = 19;
    access.y = 131.334;
    access.z = 9.9879;

}
```

While this example is not at all difficult to understand, the indirect access of union members requires a significant overhead in terms of programmer input at the keyboard.

The following program example is carried out in C++ and uses an anonymous union to accomplish the same operation.

```
int main()
{

    union {
        int x;
        float y;
        double z;
    };
```

```
    x = 19;
    y = 131.334; // value in y overwrites value in x
    z = 9.9879;  // value in z overwrites value in y


}
```

The variables x, y, and z share the same memory location and data space. Unlike unions that have tags, anonymous union values are accessed directly. This program is the equivalent of the following example.

```
int main()
{

    int *x;
    float *y;
    double *z = new double;

    y = (float *) z; // y is handed the address in z
    x = (int *) z;   // x is handed the address in z

    // x, y, and z all contain the same address
    // memory allocation is for a double type

    *x = 19;        // object value is written
    *y = 131.334;// value in y overwrites value in x
    *z = 9.9879; // value in z overwrites value in y


}
```

This works in the same manner as the previous example using the anonymous union. Here, three pointers of type int, float, and double are declared. The **new** operator is used to allocate enough memory for a double data type. Next, each of the pointers is handed the address in z. At this time, they all point to the same memory location, an area that has been allocated enough storage to contain a double-precision floating-point value. Like a union, the variables all share the same address, and memory has been allocated for the largest variable type. Also like a union, each time an object value is assigned, it overwrites the previous object value of any other variable. In a union, only one member is active at a time, and this condition has been set up in the last program by using pointers, all of which have been handed the same address. Obviously, use of the anonymous union is far more efficient, as all of the storage and addressing is handled by the union declaration. The direct access allowed by the anonymous union avoids the use of convoluted pointer operations such as those shown above.

An ANSI C programmer will initially think of the anonymous union as one that provides all of the capabilities of a standard union with no limitations. This is true in reference to ANSI C. However, C++ offers enhanced unions that may have member functions as well as data members. The anonymous union has not inherited the enhanced features of other C++ unions, so no member functions of any type are permitted.

Summary

C++ is an object-oriented language, whereas ANSI C is procedural-based. However, C++ brings with it a large set of tools that will be of immediate benefit to the programmer who is still programming without objects. These capabilities have been on the wish list of ANSI C programmers for many years and is one of the reasons why they were implemented in C++.

While it is sometimes discouraging to learn a new computer language, C++ is not entirely new to ANSI C programmers. C++ offers enough familiarity for the ANSI C programmer to be comfortable during the learning process. It also includes enough new innovations to make it highly interesting to such a programmer, and many of these new tools can be put to immediate use without drastically modifying programming style or philosophy.

The new tools offered by C++ offer advantages to programmers who wish only to continue in an enhanced style of ANSI C programming, but these advantages alone are not enough to cause most C programmers to upgrade. The main reason to switch to C++ is for programmers to gain all the advantages of OOP.

Chapter 4
++++++++++++++
Object-Oriented C++

OOP allows for the association of data structures with operations, just as our thought processes allow us to associate data we collect in our minds with other references. As human beings, we associate an object with a specific set of actions. For example, we know that an air conditioner is an electric device used for cooling. We also know that a bicycle is something that is used for transportation. There are specific things that may be done with an air conditioner that cannot be done with a bicycle. We cannot use an air conditioner for transportation and we cannot cool a room with a bicycle.

OOP allows the programmer to use similar mental processes and their associated abstract concepts within computer programs. A record can be read, altered, and saved, or high-level mathematical calculations can be performed. However, complex numbers cannot be written to files as personnel records, and personnel records cannot be used for mathematical operations, such as multiplying one record by another.

Computer languages that are procedural-based treat personnel records and complex numbers in a similar manner. An object-oriented program does not. The latter specifies acceptable behavior of its data types and allows the programmer to know exactly what may be expected from such data types.

Through OOP, it is also possible to create relationships between different data types that exhibit specific similarities. In the real world, objects and even thoughts are mentally placed into certain groupings. An earlier example of this was a car and a truck. Both exhibit similar behavior in many areas, although there are major differences in others. Using OOP, new concepts can be compared with existing concepts and decisions made based upon the relationships that come out of these comparisons.

This chapter begins the exploration of OOP using C++. The discussion of C++ functions is followed by a brief introduction to the specialized nature of C++ structures. When the two are combined, the first step is taken into the field of true OOP through a practical programming medium.

Functions in C++

While the adoption of the ANSI C standard changed the way many programmers thought about functions, C++ goes a bit farther in improving the programming and calling conventions of these entities. Most of the changes and additions are straightforward, simple, and logical. Many of the modifications common to C++ were formed specifically to address OOP. A by-product of these changes to the original ANSI C language is an increased built-in protection of data that still maintains a high degree of source-code comprehension on the part of the programmer or others who may view the code. What this means is that the structure of the language may be faithfully maintained throughout all OOP coding sequences.

Function Prototypes

C programmers who have used any of the ANSI C compilers have already encountered function prototypes. A function prototype is a declaration that defines both the return type and the parameters of a function. Using pre-ANSI C, functions were declared in the following manner.

```
int oper();
```

Such a declaration reveals nothing about the types of parameters accepted by the function. Here, the declaration merely defines the return type for the oper() function.

In C++, oper() would be prototyped using a statement similar to the one that follows.

```
int oper(char *c, double d, int i);
```

This reveals much about the function. It states that oper() is a function that returns an int value and accepts three parameters: a char pointer, a double-precision floating-point type, and an int. The compiler uses the prototype to ensure that the types of arguments passed in a function call are the same as the types of the corresponding parameters. This is what prototyping is all about, and it provides strong type-checking, something that pre-ANSI C lacked.

Without strong type-checking, it is far easier to pass illegal values to functions. A nonprototyped function might allow an int argument to be passed to a pointer parameter or to use a long int argument when a function expects a double. These kinds of errors result in invalid values for function arguments and incorrect return values from those functions. However, they generate no compiler error messages in environments that do not require or support prototyping, as was the case with the C programming language prior to ANSI C.

Unlike ANSI C, which permits the use of function prototypes, C++ requires that a function definition be made, either through the declaration of a prototype or by defining the function before it is called. In C++, prototypes do more than make sure that arguments and parameters match. An error message is generated if the compiler detects a function that does not contain a prototype or is not defined before it is called. C++ internally generates names for functions, including parameter information, which is used when several functions have the same name (function overloading).

In the function prototype for oper(), the parameter names **c**, **d**, and **i** are not stored in the symbol table, and they do not need to match the names of the corresponding parameters in the function definition. They are present solely to document the purpose of the parameters. They describe what the function parameter is expecting for an argument. In other words, the c, d, and i variable names handed to the prototype could be matched by any other names—such as f, q, and r—when the function is actually called within an application. In this usage, c, d, and i are not true variables but simply references to hold the place for true variables. Functions with an unspecified number of parameters of unknown types are declared differently in C++.

To compare, consider the following two ANSI C prototypes.

```
/* ANSI C Method */

int parse(void); /* no parameters */
int new_parse(); /* open parameter list */
```

In C++, void can be omitted and replaced with a set of empty parameters, as shown below.

```
// C++ Method

int parse(); // no parameters
int new_parse(...); // open parameter list
```

A C++ function that has an empty parameter list may not accept any arguments whatsoever. In order to have an open parameter list, the ellipses (...) must be used.

As stated earlier, all C++ functions must be prototyped (if not defined prior to their use). This means every function must have its argument list declared, and the actual definition of a function must exactly match its prototype in the number and types of parameters.

Prototyping functions creates additional work for the programmer when new source code is initially written, but prototypes are invaluable tools in preventing hard-to-find errors. These errors may require hours, days, or even weeks of debugging.

The pre-ANSI C language served as a training environment by being as rigid as possible in regard to data types passed to functions. This required the student to decipher mistakes, often through a long process of elimination. ANSI C took additional steps in the area of addressing sloppy programming, which was better, but still not good enough. C++ is expressly designed to prevent many of the problems caused by sloppy programmers passing the wrong argument type(s) to functions.

Using pre-ANSI C, programmers were accustomed to writing functions in the following manner.

```
float add(i, f);
int i;
float f;
{

        return (i + f);

}
```

While C++ will accept this form, it is considered better programming practice to use a prototype-like format for the function header. Rewriting the above function in proper C++ format would yield the following function.

```
float add(int i, float f)
{

        return( i + f);

}
```

This style is far more expressive than the now-archaic earlier method. While the standard C method of writing function headers is still supported by C++, future versions may completely drop the old C format.

Inline Functions

In properly written ANSI C programs, functions are called to provide program structure. Here, what might be called discrete operations are programmed as self-contained code blocks or functions. However, as useful as functions are, they do impose certain limits on the overall operation of a program. Arguments to functions must be pushed onto the stack prior to actually executing the function call. This and several other operations result in a sizable overhead with any function call. As a result, it is sometimes necessary to duplicate code throughout a program to increase efficiency.

This problem may be partially or wholly overcome (depending on the exact nature of the task) through the use of a C++ **inline** function. When a function definition header is preceded by the inline keyword, that function is not compiled in the same manner as standard functions. Rather, the function code is compiled and inserted into the program wherever a call to that function appears. If the function is used ten times, then the code for this function is inserted into the program ten times upon compilation, instead of just once as would be the case with a standard function. This use of the C++ inline function capability eliminates function overhead while still allowing a program to be organized in a structured manner.

The method of implementing an inline function sounds similar to a preprocessor #define in ANSI C, and this is a good parallel. An inline function does not exist as a discrete, callable routine, as is the case with a standard function. Whenever an inline function is called in a program, the compiled source code for this function is inserted at the calling point in the executable program. When compiling a program that uses inline functions, the code for the function is inserted by the compiler as though it had been placed there in its entirety by the programmer. The following program will further explain the use of inline functions.

```
#include <iostream.h>
inline void display(int a, int b)
{

    int i = (a + b) * 14;

    cout << i << endl;

}
```

```
int main()
{

    int x, y;

    x = 14;
    y = 204;

    display(x, y);

    x = 1223;
    y = 44;

    display(x, y);

}
```

The inline function named display() simply returns the sum of its two int arguments multiplied by 14. This is certainly a structured program in that functions are used to break the program down into modules. To the programmer examining this source code, there is no difference between the structure of an inline function and a standard function (other than the inline keyword). However, when this program is compiled, the following source code represents what the compiler does with the inline function.

```
int main()
{

    int x, y;

    x = 14;
    y = 204;

    int i = (x + y) * 14;

    cout << i << endl;
```

```
x = 1223;
y = 44;

int i = (x + y) * 14;

cout << i << endl;


}
```

Admittedly, display() is a frivolous function that adds its two arguments, multiplies them by 14, and then writes this value to the screen, but it serves its purpose as an easily understood example for explaining inline functions.

It can be seen that the inline function concept can be closely equated with a #define preprocessor definition. Naturally, inline functions will increase the size of the compiled program, but this increase is offset by a decrease in processing overhead. All inline functions must be defined prior to the program point in which they are used, due to the fact that their source code must be precompiled before it can be inserted into the program.

A major drawback when using inline functions is the inherent increase in program size. Simple functions, such as display(), are easily adapted to inline definitions, but complex inline functions may contain a substantial amount of code. It is necessary for the programmer to be aware of the program size overhead that comes with the use of inline functions. In some instances, inline definitions are preferred. In others, the program-size overhead is too great a price to pay for a minimal amount of execution-speed increase. If a program is becoming a liability due to slow execution speed, it's simple to re-declare any suspect functions as inline. It is also necessary to move the source code of these functions to a point in the program prior to their being called.

There is a limit on the number of inline functions that can be used in any one program. The exact number will depend on the total size of all inline functions and the amount of available memory. The inline keyword means that the function will be an inline type only if it can be accommodated. Due to this limitation, using the inline keyword does not absolutely guarantee that the function will be an inline type. The compiler will make the effort, but if an additional inline function cannot be accommodated, it will be invoked as a standard function. If a program calls too many inline functions, it will stop inlining altogether when it runs short of memory. Any inline functions may be compiled as regular functions.

In general, inline functions are usually small functions with minimal source code. There are also a few restrictions, as none of the iteration control statements can be used. This means no **for**, **while,** or **do-while** loops are permitted in the body of an in line function.

Function Argument Default Values

In ANSI C, a function that expects an argument must have one, or an error occurs, either during compilation or by returning an erroneous value when the function is actually executed. This is an appropriate response in many programming situations. In others, programming tasks could be addressed more quickly if the compiler were (somehow) told that if an argument is not provided, it should default to some predetermined value. The great advantage of C++ is that it allows for setting default values, values that will be used whenever a function, so programmed, is called without an argument.

The following function serves as an example.

```
#include <iostream.h>
void beep(int beepno);   //prototype
int main()
{

    beep(1);
    beep(10);

void beep(int beepno)
{

    int i;
    long delay;

    for (i = 1; i <= beepno; ++i) { //number of beeps
        cout  << char(7)    // Beep character
        for  (delay = 1; delay <= 100000; ++delay)
            ;                    //delay between beeps


    }


}
```

This function sends the beep character (ASCII 7) to be written to the console, broadcasting a 1000-Hertz tone through the computer speaker. This is accomplished using the cout stream and casting the value of 7 to type char. An int argument that determines the number of times the beep is sounded is passed to the function. Beep() is called twice by the program. Each time beep() is called, it must be handed an argument to determine the number of beeps that are to be sounded. When using this function often, a programmer might find that only one beep is required in most situations. It becomes a minor inconvenience to constantly supply an argument of 1 each time such a call is made. The solution might be to write a new function called beep1() that requires no argument (void) and will sound a single beep each time it is called. The original beep() function would be called only when numerous beeps were needed. Using C++, however, it is simple to use the original beep() function by utilizing the default argument value feature provided by this language.

Because it has been determined that most of the time beep() is called with an argument value of 1, it would facilitate programming if the function could be written in such a manner that it would sound only a single beep if it is supplied no argument. Should an argument be supplied, then it would be incorporated into the function. The following program does this and requires only a simple change to the earlier function example.

```cpp
#include <iostream.h>
void beep(int beepno = 1); // Default Value prototype
int main()
{

    beep();   // No argument-Default to 1
    beep(10);

}
void beep(int beepno)
{

    int i
    long delay;

    for (i = 0; i < beepno; ++i) {
        cout << char(7);
        for (delay = 0; delay <= 18000; ++delay)
            ;
    }

}
```

The only change to this example is in the prototype. A value of 1 is assigned as the default for beepno. This means that any time beep() is called without an argument, the default value of 1 will be in effect. In the executable portion of the program, beep() has been called twice. The first call does not pass an argument to the function; therefore, the default value of 1 is handed to beep(). The second time this same function is called, an argument value of 10 is passed to beep(). This value is handed to the function and the default value is ignored.

Setting the default value is accomplished in the function prototype and not in the function definition proper. The C++ compiler will use the function prototype to build a call in the event that the function is invoked without an argument.

Overloading

Overloading is the act of using one name to perform two or more different operations. The concept of overloading was introduced in a previous chapter. With overloading in C++, a single function name or operator can be used to invoke numerous processes, each of which serves a different purpose. While initially confusing to persons learning C++, this is a tool necessary to accomplish true OOP.

In ANSI C, a function is a unique entity. Each function will have its own individual name and no other function may have that same name. However, sometimes the one function/one name aspect of ANSI C can hinder efficiency by adding unnecessary work for the programmer. As an example, ANSI C has several intrinsic functions that return the absolute value of a numeric argument. Each of these has a different name to reflect the type of numeric value that is returned. All of these functions perform the same basic operation, but their return and argument data types are different. The following ANSI C functions will begin the discussion on function overloading.

```
int isquare(int x)
{

    return(x * x);

}

double dsquare(double d)
```

```
{

    return(d * d);

}
```

These two functions return the square of their arguments. They have this feature in common. However, the isquare() function accepts an int argument and returns an int data type. The dsquare() function accepts a double argument value and returns this same type. In ANSI C, each function must have an exclusive name that is not shared by any other function. For this reason, isquare() is the function that returns the square of an int argument, and dsquare() returns the square of a double argument.

Through C++ function overloading, both of these functions may be given the same name while still assuring that each retains its own operational individuality. The following C++ program does this.

```
#include <iostream.h>
int square(int i);
double square(double d);

int main()
{

    int x;
    double z;

    x = square(25);
    z = square(128.39264);

    cout << x << " " << z << endl;

}
int square(int i)
{

    return(i * i);

}
double square(double d)
{
    return(d * d);

}
```

This program calls two different functions that have the same name, square(). The only alteration made to the original function source code has been to change the name of each to square() and provide the prototypes. This program takes advantage of C++ function overloading.

The function prototypes specify different argument types for each function. One version of square() requires an int argument, while the other needs a double-precision floating-point argument. This is all the information that the C++ compiler needs to determine which function is actually being called within the program.

The C++ compiler makes this determination based on argument evaluation. If a function named square() is called with an int argument, then the function that was originally named isquare() in the ANSI C example is accessed. Arguments to square() of type double access the function formerly named dsquare().

Once the overloaded functions have been written, the programmer no longer needs to be concerned with function name selection, as the compiler will determine which function will be called. From this point on in the program, the programmer needs only to be aware of the fact that square() is a function that returns the square of its argument (int or double). Of course, the programmer must be fully aware of the return expected for this value to be utilized by the remainder of the program.

In the above example, the function returns are assigned to common variables that serve as arguments that are sent to the output stream for screen display. However, if printf() were used for display purposes, it would be necessary to supply a %d specification for the int-return version of square() and a %lf specification for the double-return version. This points to the fact that function overloading in no way relieves the programmer from the responsibility of data type knowledge. Overloading simply allows one name to be used for several functions, each of which accepts a different type of argument. Three functions with the same name still represent three different functions. The fact that they can be called by the same name does nothing to mitigate the fact that three different functions exist and that each may have a different return value.

The parameters of the function arguments are the key to the compiler's determining which overloaded function is to be called. The return type is of no consequence as a determinate. This means that overloaded functions must contain different argument types and/or numbers of arguments. Take the following declarations as an example.

```
int add(int x, int y);
int add(int, x, int y, int z);
```

Both are acceptable, as they can be differentiated by the number of arguments they require. However, the following declarations are unacceptable.

```
int add(int x, int y);
double add(int i, int j);
```

These would result in an 'ambiguity' error when compilation is attempted. While each of these prototypes returns a different data type, they both require the same types and numbers of arguments. The C++ compiler cannot distinguish between the two, so the compile process fails.

Recall in the earlier discussion on C++ streams that the get() function was obviously overloaded, since it could be used in two different manners to invoke two completely separate processes. It could be assumed that one version of get would be prototyped or defined in the following manner

```
get(char *, int, char);
```

while the other function would be prototyped as shown below.

```
get(char);
```

These functions exhibit completely different argument parameters, which is absolutely essential for overloading to work.

Prototypes are not required for function overloading, as long as the function is fully defined prior to its use, as is the case with all other functions in C++. Therefore, the following usage is perfectly legal.

```
int recip(int i)  // return reciprocal of int arg
{

    return(-i);

}

long recip(long r) // return reciprocal of long arg
{

    return(-r);

}
```

```
int main()
{

    // remainder of C++ program that calls recip()
```

In this example, the overloaded functions have been defined prior to usage, and prototyping is unnecessary. The recip() overloaded function returns the reciprocal of its argument. If the argument is an int, then the first function is called. If it is a long int, the second is accessed. But what happens if the argument to recip is a char as is shown below?

```
int x = recip('A');
```

No function has been defined to accept a char argument. However, the compiler will cause the int version of recip to be called, since this is the version that offers the easiest conversion. This call will result in int x being assigned a value of –65, the reciprocal of ASCII 65 represented by the char value 'A'. The following call will result in an ambiguity error.

```
int x = recip(351.65);
```

The error occurs because both versions of recip() require an int argument. If recip() were not an overloaded function, the conversion of the floating-point value to its int equivalent would take place. However, since recip() is overloaded, no (internal) conversion is possible.

When overloaded functions contain default values, special consideration is necessary. For instance, the following function prototypes present no problem at all.

```
int smash(int x);

int smash(int x, int y);
```

The argument parameters for the functions named smash() are completely different. The compiler will have no problem in sorting out calls to functions of this type. However, the following prototypes won't work.

```
int smash(int x);
int smash(int x, int y = 124);
```

The reason for this should be obvious. The compiler won't be able to distinguish between a call to the function represented by the first prototype and a call to the second. Since the second function prototype contains a default value for its second argument, a call to this function might include only a single argument with the other defaulting to the value of 124. The other requires only a single argument. There would be no way of knowing which function was being accessed if the latter was called with only a single argument, depending upon the default to supply the other.

It is acceptable to provide overloaded functions with default values, as long as no use of these defaults during a function call can result in an identity crisis. It is not the actual call that creates the error but the possibility that an ambiguous call could be made that causes the compiler to fail.

Function overloading in C++ is a highly useful tool. However, it should be used sparingly and only where appropriate. For instance, it would be highly undesirable to overload a function named add() so that, rather than returning the sum of two int arguments, it returned the difference of two double arguments. This would be totally ridiculous, hindering programming efficiency rather than aiding it. Even though it can be done, it makes no sense to do it. Indeed, function overloading has been put to some absolutely horrible uses, completely obliterating source-code comprehension. Remember, function overloading is a logical method of calling by one name several functions that perform the same basic types of operations.

Operator Overloading

Just as overloaded functions have identical names and may be called upon to invoke different processes, the same is true of operators. Overloaded operators work on the same principle as overloaded functions. The compiler is able to determine which operator process is being called by examining the parameters of the call, the number and types of arguments or operands.

The operators in ANSI C are fixed, in that they are an integral part of the language, and there is no mechanism by which these operator

processes can be altered or redefined. However, C++ offers the programmer the capability of giving additional new definitions to the existing operator set. Operator overloading is a process where existing
operators are attached to new processes, allowing them to function in a
user-defined manner.

It is easy for programmers to consciously lose track of just how valuable operators are. The mathematical operators such as +, −, *, and / actually represent predefined actions that are carried out through special
functions. Languages that do not allow for such operators are forced to
perform these processes by means of function calls alone.

```
z = x + y;
```

This simple assignment line depends on the addition operator to call up
a function that will add the values in the two variables. Without such
operators, the above assignment might look like the following.

```
z = add(x, y);
```

Even the assignment operator (=) performs a relatively complex function
by writing the object value into the memory location assigned to the (z)
variable.

It is also important to realize that most persons tend to think of these
operators as non-type-specific. In the expression z = x + y, it makes no
difference whether variables x and y are floats, longs, doubles, chars, or
ints. The function version above would be far more demanding as to
data type. The code that is generated by z = x + y, where x, y, and z are
int data types, will be quite different than if the three variables were
floats.

The C++ programmer can overload operators using a method that is
similar to function overloading. A (usually) small amount of code is tied
to an operator symbol. Whenever this operator is invoked in a manner
that distinguishes it from the intrinsic (built-in) operator process, this
function is executed with the arguments or operands provided.

All C++ operators may be overloaded, with the following exceptions.

```
.     .*     ::     ?:
```

Any attempts to overload these operators will result in an error. This same restriction also applies to the preprocessor symbols of # and ##. Other than these few exceptions, all operators may be overloaded.

At this point, it is necessary to differentiate between operators and symbols. It has been necessary to use the term *symbol* when introducing operator overloading; however, don't get the idea that a symbol can be overloaded. Only operators are overloaded. A unary operator has one parameter such as *x, &x, ++y, y--, etc. A binary operator has two parameters, as shown by the examples that follow.

```
x * y      a + b      i % h
```

These operators remain binary or unary whenever they are overloaded. Therefore, a unary operator cannot be used as a binary operator. If symbols (as opposed to operators) were involved, then just about anything desired could be done with them (as is the case with a function name when programming overloaded functions). If an intrinsic operator is overloaded, the new process must still take the original form (binary/unary) of the operator.

Common unary operators are shown below.

```
&   *   !   ~   -   (cast type)   sizeof
```

All overloaded unary operators must return a value that is of the same type as their single argument. The (cast type) operator must return a type that is the same as the type found in parentheses.

All binary operators require two arguments. The binary operators are shown below.

```
+   -   /   *   %   <   >   <<   >>   <=   >=
            ,      ==   &&   !=   ^   |   ||
```

The following assignment operators are also considered to be special unary types having only one argument.

```
=   +=   -=   /=   *=   %=   <<=   >>=   &=   ^=   |=
```

Unlike the standard unary operators, assignment operators are not limited as to return value type when overloaded.

Operator overloading offers many advantages. However, it can only be used with derived data types such as the new data types created by a struct or class. A new process cannot be assigned to an operator and have this process apply to intrinsic data types such as int, float, double, char, etc. Operator overloading can only be applied to derived data types and objects in C++. If it is assumed that a struct named *numbers* is declared in C++, then its contents are said to be of type **numbers**. Even though this struct will contain (internally) conventional data types, the struct is a derived type that can be identified by its name, in this case, *numbers*. This is the class of data that overloaded operators can address.

The following programs provide a brief introduction to the programming overloaded operator functions.

```c
/* ANSI C Program */
/* Sum the data members of two structs and write */
/* the result to the members of a third struct */

struct numbers {     /* Struct Template */
    int x, y;  /* Struct members */
};

#include <stdio.h>
main()
{

    numbers a, b, c;

    a.x = 10;
    a.y = 15;

    b.x = 20;
    b.y = 25;

    c.x = a.x + b.x;  /* Summing Sequence */
    c.y = a.y + b.y;  /* Summing Sequence */

    printf("%d  %d\n", c.x, c.y);

}
```

This program will display the following values on the screen.

$$30 \quad 45$$

These values represent a.x + b.x and a.y + b.y.

This is an ANSI C program that declares three variables to be of type **numbers**. This is a derived (non-intrinsic) data type, so the data members are accessed via the struct member (.) operator. The two int members within **numbers a** and **numbers b** are assigned values. The next operation effectively assigns to the **numbers c** data elements the sum of the respective data elements in **a** and **b**.

All operations performed on derived data types in ANSI C are laborious in that the data members must be individually accessed each time an operation is to be performed. However, an ANSI C function could be written that would handle the summing operation. Basically, it would consist of the two-line code sequence labeled "Summing Sequence" in the program above, but it would be far better to somehow use the addition operator (+) in the same manner that it is used with intrinsic data types—if only this could be done.

C++ allows this to be accomplished through operator overloading. When function and operator overloading are coupled with C++ structs or classes, the real power of overloading becomes apparent. The following C++ program does exactly what the ANSI C version did, but in a manner more in line with OOP technique.

```
struct numbers {     // Struct template
    int x, y;     // Struct members
};

// Operator Function
numbers operator + (numbers i, numbers h)
{

    numbers hold;

    hold.x = i.x + h.x;
    hold.y = i.y + h.y;
    return(hold);

}
```

```
#include <iostream.h>
int main()
{

    numbers a, b, c;

    a.x = 10;
    a.y = 15;

    b.x = 20;
    b.y = 25;

    c = a + b; // Add using operator function

    cout << c.x << "  " << c.y << endl;

}
```

It is stressed that the use of iostream.h in this example in no way affects the operator overloading. The printf() function and standard stdio.h conventions could be used as in the ANSI C example.

The major changes in this program over the former (ANSI C) example are highlighted. This is an example of operator overloading. An operator function is declared in much the same manner as a standard function. It includes a return of type **numbers**, the function name, the argument list, and the source code for the function. The following code is a reproduction of the operator function.

```
// Operator Function

numbers operator + (numbers i, numbers h)
{

    numbers hold;

        hold.x = i.x + h.x;
        hold.y = i.y + h.y;
        return(hold);

}
```

The return type is **numbers**, a derived type. Where the name of a standard function would normally be found, there is instead the + operator, preceded by the **operator** keyword. This keyword identifies an operator function that returns a value of type **numbers**. Whenever any operator function is written, the operator keyword must be a part of the definition.

The rest of the function is standard. Within its body, another variable of type **numbers** is declared, and the first data element in this variable is assigned the sum of the first data element values in **i** and **h**. The same thing is done for the second data elements in the set. Finally, the loaded struct value is passed back to the calling program.

Since the + operator is a binary type in its intrinsic form, it is also a binary type in overloaded form. This means that two operands or arguments are required. Their values are passed to variables **i** and **h** in the operator function.

Within the calling program, the following expression is found.

```
c = a + b;
```

The + operator is the overloaded operator function that is identified by the compiler, as it has two operands of type **numbers**. This differentiates it from the intrinsic addition operator. The end result is the summing of two derived data types and returning the value to another derived type. This process mimics the operation of the intrinsic addition operator and is more logical from a programming point of view. It can be seen that the operator function is little more than a standard function body that is invoked by an operator instead of by an orthodox function name.

Any binary operator could have been substituted for the + operator, and the program would still work in the same manner. However, this could create all kinds of understanding problems. Since the purpose of the operator function was to add derived data types, the addition operator was the logical choice for overloading. If the subtraction (−) operator were chosen, there would be absolutely no change in the end result of this program, providing that the operator function code body was left intact, but this would be extremely poor programming practice because it would tend to confuse anyone viewing the source code, including the original programmer.

It is necessary to realize that the examples in this text are made as elementary and unencumbered as possible to facilitate understanding. However, actual coding practices typically involve hundreds or even thousands of code lines. It is not unusual for a programmer to get bogged down in his or her own code as the complexity increases. Therefore, it is mandatory from a personal programming standpoint to write code that is straightforward and understandable. Using the overloaded subtraction operator to add two entities is a decidedly bad programming practice.

The rule of thumb in operator overloading is to maintain the basic process for which the intrinsic operator was designed. This will lead to far less confusion and make operator overloading a programming boon instead of a confusing maze of symbols.

C++ Structs and Function Calls

When working with structs in ANSI C, even simple operations may be quite clumsy. It is in this area that C++ overloaded functions and operators can be used to allow the programmer a more direct approach. Overloading is absolutely essential to the manipulation of C++ objects (classes). Without overloading, true OOP cannot be achieved with any degree of practicality.

C++ structs offer several advantages when compared with their ANSI C counterparts. Structs in this newer language are often referred to as *enhanced*, since they allow for a far more elaborate range of operations. An ANSI C struct contains data elements that are grouped as a single unit. Only data elements, also known as data members, are allowed in an ANSI C struct. However, C++ structs allow for the inclusion of functions. These member functions have a special relationship with the struct data members and allow for a great deal more efficiency in handling struct data because of the high degree of encapsulation possible in combining data members and member functions. *These are the beginnings of an object-oriented approach.*

Previous program examples have shown how functions and/or operators with the same name or symbol can be called upon to perform different processes. The last program showed an example of operator overloading using the + operator to perform addition on derived (nonintrinsic) data types. The next program follows a similar line of attack, but it also includes a member function to handle the task of making assignments to the struct data members.

```
struct numbers {
    int x, y;

};
```

```
// This function assigns data members
inline numbers assign(int i, int h)
{
    numbers hold;

    hold.x = i;
    hold.y = h;

    return(hold);

}

numbers operator + (numbers a, numbers b); // function prototype

#include <iostream.h>
int main()
{

    numbers a, b, c;

    a = assign(10, 15);
    b = assign(20, 25);
    c = a + b;

    cout << c.x << "   " << c.y << endl;

}
numbers operator + (numbers i, numbers h)
{

    numbers hold;

    hold.x = i.x + h.x;
    hold.y = i.y + h.y;

    return(hold);
}
```

The major differences in this program have been highlighted. Using a function to load values into the data members of an array is not an exclusive C++ feature, as this can be as easily done in ANSI C as well.

However, this program uses an **inline** function, a feature that is available only in C++. Inline functions were covered in Chapter 2.

It is appropriate to use an inline function here, because the assign() function code is quite compact. The **inline** keyword tells the C++ compiler that the function is to be made inline (if possible). The operator function is still a part of this program, but it has been prototyped since its definition has been moved to the end of the source-code chain. The assign() function simply writes its arguments into the data members of the struct.

The executable code within main() has now become more compact. A function has been provided to load data into the data members, and an operator function (+) is provided to allow the data to be addressed by a familiar mathematical operator. Admittedly, the code outside of main() is becoming larger, but this is done to provide more tools for manipulating the struct data. If twenty struct variables were involved (instead of three), then the increased efficiency regarding the calls made under main() would be far more obvious.

Now that a single operator function has been explored, it's time to begin thinking about other operator functions that can perform additional operations on derived data types. The following operator functions expand the struct by encoding subtraction and multiplication capabilities into the original program.

```
numbers operator - (numbers i, numbers h)
{

    numbers hold;

    hold.x = i.x - h.x;
    hold.y = i.y - h.y;

    return(hold);

}

numbers operator * (numbers i, numbers h)
{

        numbers hold;

    hold.x = i.x * h.x;
    hold.y = i.y * h.y;
```

```
        return(hold);


}
```

When these operator functions are #included with the original program, the following statements will work in the same manner as the original + operator function, except they will perform multiplication and subtraction operations.

```
                        z = x * y;
                        z = x - y;
```

Each of these operator functions forms a very useful tool, especially when highly complex processes are involved. The examples in this chapter are quite simple in order to painlessly introduce the reader to this new concept. However, operator functions can grow to larger proportions when the applications they address demand such capabilities.

All of the functions discussed to this point address derived data types. However, none of them are actual members of the struct. The functions received struct arguments and returned struct values, but they were all external to the structure, proper.

C++ allows structures and classes to have their own member functions along with data elements. The source code that follows eliminates the external assign() function and replaces it with a **member function**, one that is declared within the struct.

```
struct numbers {
    int x, y;
    void assign(int i, int j); // member function prototype

};

numbers operator + (numbers a, numbers b); // function prototype

#include <iostream.h>
int main()
{

    numbers a, b, c;
```

```
    a.assign(10, 15);
    b.assign(20, 25);

    c = a + b;

    cout << c.x << "   " << c.y << endl;

}

void numbers::assign(int i, int j)
{
    numbers hold;

    x = i;
    y = j;

}
numbers operator + (numbers i, numbers h)
{

    numbers hold;

    hold.x = i.x + h.x;
    hold.y = i.y + h.y;

    return(hold);

}
```

This program differs from the former only in the exact method used to
make assignments. Note that assign() is declared within the struct. This
means that it is a **member function** of the struct named **numbers**. It
is prototyped for a void return, for it will make direct assignments to the
struct data elements as opposed to returning a value to a struct target.
    The assign() function definition is shown below.

```
        void numbers::assign(int i, int j)
        {

            numbers hold;

            x = i;
            y = j;

        }
```

The function is declared within the **numbers** struct, so it is not directly accessible by program elements that lie outside of the struct. The scope resolution operator (::) is used with the struct name as a means of access. The following definition line means that a function declared within the scope of struct **numbers** returns a void type and accepts two ints as argument values.

```
void numbers::assign(int i, int j)
```

Within the function body, the data elements in the struct are directly accessed via their names (x and y). These elements are assigned the values in argument variables **i** and **j**.

When the member function is called from the program portion under main(), a familiar format is used.

```
a.assign(10, 15);
b.assign(20, 25);
```

Function access in C++ uses the structure member (.) operator, the same method used in ANSI C to access data elements. Since the C++ enhanced struct can have its own member functions, it makes sense to access them in this fashion. The argument values to this function are assigned to the data elements in the respective struct variables.

At this point a glimmering of true OOP begins to surface. In this example, a discrete object in the form of a struct is manipulated as an object and not just a collection of intrinsic data types. Through the use of operator and member functions, the object is addressed as a very unique entity. It has its own function for assignment and even its own operator for internal mathematics. The assign() function and the operator function will not work with any other object. Both can be used only by the numbers object.

At the beginning of this book, we stated that an object is a unique entity that accomplishes its operations internally. Its personality determines what it can and cannot do, and all of its operations are internal to the object. As the previous examples have built up to the one just presented, readers can see that the personality of this simple object involves assignment and mathematical manipulation. Each of these processes is internal, a part of the personality of the object. The methods of accomplishing assignment and mathematical operations are determined internally by the object and not by some outside entity such as the intrinsic assignment operator (=) or by intrinsic mathematical operators. Each operation is exclusive to the object.

However, a considerable journey remains before entering fully into the realm of true OOP. While it is true that assign() and the + operator function will work only with the numbers object, it is also true that access to the object from outside its scope (outside of the object, proper) by other functions and operators can be had at any time. In OOP, a true object is accessed only by its own functions and operators—that is, everything that can be done with the object is determined by what is actually contained within the object. In this example, the assign() function can address the struct data members because it is a member function declared from within the struct. However, the data members can also be addressed by conventional methods under main(), as shown by the two assignment lines.

```
a.x = 10;
a.y = 15;
```

No exclusivity is granted when using structs because access to the struct is public by default. This means that any function or operator that knows the struct name and data element names can access them. The public nature of struct data does not allow for pure OOP operations. For this reason, structs should not be used as objects. In C++, structs and classes have many similarities, but classes are the true objects, while enhanced structs are used for more traditional (non-object-oriented) purposes akin to their usage in ANSI C.

Summary

The discussions in this chapter have allowed the reader to enter the outside perimeter of true OOP. The special usage of functions in C++ is a prerequisite to continuing with the object-oriented aspects of this language.

Function overloading and operator overloading are indispensable in reaching a goal of addressing objects as unique entities instead of as collections of common data elements. The operations discussed here have begun to concentrate on the collection as a unit instead of the individual elements that make up that collection. In order to do this, the C++ function and operator overloading capabilities have been relied on heavily, along with the expanded C++ struct. The next chapter takes up immediately where this one leaves off, as the reader fully enters the arena of OOP.

Chapter 5

++++++++++++++

C++ Classes: The True Objects in Object-Oriented Programming

Previous discussions have formed the framework to allow for a fuller understanding of the object-oriented tools offered by C++. This knowledge will enhance the reader's grasp of the mechanics needed to use the OOP concept for true object-oriented programming. This chapter introduces the reader to the mechanics of classes and the concept of object manipulation. The programming tools will not be especially foreign, because of the preparation provided in earlier chapters. However, grasping the full concept of OOP may take a bit longer. Throughout the discussions that follow, remember that OOP is based on the data (object) operated on as opposed to the operations themselves. The discussions and program examples that follow are designed to give the reader an encapsulated mental picture of what this programming method entails.

C++ Classes

OOP via C++ involves classes. A C++ class is the true object in OOP. It is a user-defined type. In ANSI C, a new data type is subject to the rules of usage of standard (intrinsic) data types. This is not entirely true in C++, where the programmer is allowed to define not only the contents of a class but also the behavior of that class. To ANSI C programmers, a class is a new entity, not offered in C.

Mastering the concept and usage of classes is crucial to learning C++, but it is not as difficult as it might first appear. To this point, the reader has been introduced to overloaded functions and operators and to the concept of the member function, as used with C++ enhanced structs. These enhancements allow the programmer to define object behavior. While there are many operational similarities between structs and classes, they are entirely different in concept. Such differences may seem subtle at this point in the learning process. However, understand that classes are traditionally used for an OOP approach while C++ structs are used for procedural-based operations.

A class object should be thought of as a unique entity, unlike any other data type. The class is the object in OOP, and such an object determines its own rules of behavior based on the way the programmer writes these rules into the class object. An object actually allows itself to be created (and destroyed). The exact nature of its creation is contained within the class, proper. The class also determines how it may (and may not) be manipulated. Access to the components of the class object are governed by the rules that are defined and contained within the class. Generally, a class may not be accessed by the built-in operators and functions in the C++ language unless it allows for such access.

The class object may even be thought of as a mini-world. It contains its own rules of natural order, access, manipulation, and interaction. It may even pass on some or all of these properties to another class object, which is said to inherit from the original or base class.

Member Access Control

One of the first things that must be learned about a class is that, by default, all of its contents are private. This means that they cannot be accessed by any operator or function that is not specifically a part of that class (or granted special access privileges). This is not true of a struct whose members are public by default and may be accessed by any program element (i.e., from any **scope**) that has the name of the struct. The following program will demonstrate the private nature of the contents of a class.

```
// NOTE: This program is defective and will not
// compile.

class alpha {     // declare a class named "alpha"

    int a, b;     // a & b are members of this class

};
```

```
int main()
{

    alpha tap;

    tap.a = 10;
    tap.b = 15;


}
```

This program cannot be compiled because it contains errors. However, noting these errors is important because they represent the errors ANSI C programmers often make when learning the object-oriented approach of C++.

Many of the same terms are used when addressing classes that apply in addressing structs. Most of the same operators apply as well. In the above example, a class object of type alpha is created within the program under control of main() in the same manner a struct variable would be declared. There are operational similarities between structs and classes, so the mechanics shouldn't be foreign to the ANSI C programmer. However, the concepts are completely different, so don't make too many assumptions about a class object and its relationship to a struct.

In this example, int a and b are members of the class named alpha. Within the program, **tap**, an object of class alpha, is declared. However, this program will not work at all. It won't even compile, for the data members of the class cannot be assigned in any way, shape, or form using any standard operator or function. The reason for this lies in the fact that the members of a class are private by default. They can be accessed only by a member function contained within the class (or by other functions that are granted special access permission). The control of access to class contents is a mandatory feature of OOP.

Any class object is a unique entity, unlike any other object. The methods by which an object is manipulated are determined internally, within the object. If all functions, operators, or programs can access an object in any way, then the unique characteristics of the object are lost. The object-oriented nature of the program are gone. In OOP, the object determines how it is manipulated. This type of determination can be maintained only by incorporating strict (inner-object) access control. In this example, no member functions are defined within the class or declared within its body, so there is absolutely no way the class members can be accessed. This is a completely useless program.

Trying to use a class in the manner shown above is nonsensical. This is not OOP; it is an attempt at standard, procedural-based programming that is used in ANSI C. In true OOP, the procedures are determined by the object's characteristics and not so much by the language.

Object access control is essential to the very concept of OOP. In the previous example, variables that may contain integer values are involved. However, real-world objects such as airplanes, dogs, cats, people, and places are often involved in OOP. We can't take the square root of an airplane and we certainly cannot add a person to a cat and arrive at a mathematical sum that has any real meaning.

C++ offers three member access specifiers, each or all of which may be actively used within a class.

```
                    ACCESS SPECIFIERS

                        private
                        protected
                        public
```

The class members that follow each of these specifiers are said to have a different level of access.

Since C++ classes default to private, the private access specifier is not specifically required. The class in the program example above could also have been written in the following manner.

```
                class alpha {
                     private:
                     int a, b;

                };
```

This won't change anything, as the private access specifier is the default condition of the class members. This example simply spells out what had already taken place by default. Whenever an access specifier is used, all member declarations or definitions that appear following it fall under that mode of access. This mode remains in effect until a different specifier is used to change the access mode of the declarations and definitions that, in turn, follow it. When access is private, only member functions of the class may access any other member function or data member unless special access privileges are granted to some other function or entity. This latter concept will be discussed in the Chapter 6.

The term *member function* is often done away with completely in OOP and replaced by the more appropriate term *method* to describe members of a class that are called on to manipulate class contents. *Member function* and *method* are synonymous as they relate to the class object.

If the *public* access specifier is used (in place of *private* as shown above), this means that all of the members defined or declared after the specifier are governed by the public access mode. This allows outside entities to directly use or manipulate the members. This would allow the original program example to do what is intended, but it definitely would not be an object-oriented approach. Private access is the default for C++ classes, while public access is the default for C++ structs.

Protected mode is the same as private in many respects, but this mode also allows access by methods that are derived from the declared class. The subject of class derivations and protected access mode will be fully discussed in a later chapter. For now, it can be accurately stated that protected access will grant access to some entities while completely denying access to others.

In OOP, it is customary for *all data members of a class to be private*, enabling them to be accessed only by methods (member functions) of that class. Class methods may be private in some cases and public in others, depending on how the programmer wishes to control access. It is also customary to include the private keyword even when it is the default condition in order to provide more program expression.

Using Classes

The following program will take the reader a bit farther into the realm of OOP by creating class objects and manipulating a small number of data.

```
#include <iostream.h>
#include <string.h>

class person {
    private:
        int age;
        char name[50];
    public:
        void assign(int x, char *c);
        void display(void);

};
```

```
int main()
{

    person male, female;

    male.assign(27, "Frank E. Jones");
    female.assign(24, "Mary F. Grayson");

    male.display();
    female.display();

}
void person::assign(int i, char *s) {

    age = i;
    strcpy(name, s);

}
void person::display(void)
{

    cout << name << " is " << age << " years old." << endl;

}
```

When executed, the program will display the following information on the monitor screen.

```
            Frank E. Jones is 27 Years old.
            Mary F. Grayson is 24 years old.
```

This program creates two objects named **male** and **female**. These are objects of class **person**. This code probably looks quite foreign, but breaking it down into manageable blocks will reveal that it is not all that unusual or complex. Discussing this example in terms of small code blocks should provide the reader with a better grasp of the intent of each major component. The class structure is shown below.

```
class person {
    private:
        int age;
        char name[50];
    public:
        void assign(int x, char *c);
        void display(void);

};
```

Note that an int variable (**age**) and a char array (**name**) are declared. The private keyword is used (although this default condition would exist without it) to restrict access to these two data members to methods (member functions) of class **person**. This means that only the methods of the **person** class may gain access to these two members.

The **public** keyword is also used in the person class. Here, two method (member function) prototypes are found. The two methods, assign() and display(), are declared public, so that they may be used outside of the class scope (called from main(), i.e.). However, these two methods only address the private data members of class **person**. In other words, they can be called from outside of the class, but they will only address **person** objects.

The source code for the two class methods is shown below.

```
void person::assign(int i, char *s)
{
    age = i;
    strcpy(name, s);

}

void person::display(void)
{

    cout << name << " is " << age << " years old." << endl;

}
```

Both of these methods are declared void because no return would be expected. Note that each is accessed via the scope resolution operator. The following expression means that a method named assign() returns a void data type and is contained within the scope of a class named **person**.

```
void person::assign(int i, char *s)
```

A similar member function was presented in Chapter 3, and although the assignment types are different, the mechanics of this method are the same. The values contained in **i** and **s** are assigned directly (by name) to class data members age and name[]. The direct access of these data members is possible only because assign() has been prototyped in the **person** class.

The same is true of the display() method. It writes the contents of name[] and age directly to the output stream. Notice again that the class data members are accessed directly.

The display() and assign() methods offer the only means of accessing the data members of the **person** class, because these are the only methods that are part of the **person** object. Performing other manipulations on these **private** data members would require that additional methods be provided as part of the class.

Under the auspices of main(), two objects named **male** and **female** are created, as shown in the program fragments below.

```
int main()
{

    person male, female;

    male.assign(27, "Frank E. Jones");
    female.assign(24, "Mary F. Grayson");

    male.display();
    female.display();

}
```

They are of type **person**. The assign() method is accessed via the member-of operator, and the **age** value and **name** are assigned. Next, the display() method is accessed in the same manner, displaying the desired information on the monitor. Each object of type **person** has handled its own assignment and display.

This example has demonstrated object manipulation in an object-oriented manner. The data members and the methods are all a part of the object. The person object is a unique entity that contains unique tools (methods) for assignment and display. All of these have combined to form a true C++ object.

Constructors

Every C++ class has a constructor and a destructor. If not explicitly programmed, a single constructor and destructor are generated by default. A constructor is a special function that is a class member bearing the same name as the class. Its purpose is to build objects. A constructor is called within the program to allocate space for an object, assign values to the object's data members, and perform general housekeeping tasks.

There may be any number of constructors in a given class, but a class will have at least one, even if it is generated by the compiler through default. The constructor will have the same name as the class, so in order to choose which constructor to call, the compiler compares the arguments used in the object declaration with the constructor parameter list. This concept is not new and is the same as the process used to choose between overloaded functions/operators.

Constructors are quite similar to other functions. However, while they may have parameters like any other function, they cannot return a value. This restriction is imposed because constructors are usually called when defining a new object when there is no way to retrieve or examine any return value.

If a constructor is not explicitly programmed, then the compiler creates one for each class. This is the default constructor and it has no arguments. Its purpose is to place values of zero in every byte of the object's variables. When a constructor is supplied by the programmer, the default constructor is not generated.

In the previous program example, a constructor was not explicitly programmed. This means that data member assignments were handled by a default constructor that simply initialized all data members to zero. The assign() method was used to initialize the class data members. This was a constructor, as it has already been learned that a constructor has the same name as the class. The following program is an expansion of the last example that includes an explicit constructor for the **person** class, thus providing for initialization to be made on declaration of the class object.

```
#include <iostream.h>
#include <string.h>
class person {
    private:
        int age;
    char name[50];
    public:
        person(int x, char *c); //Constructor
        void display(void);
};

int main()
{

    person male(27, "Frank E. Jones");
    person female(24, "Mary F. Grayson");

    male.display();
    female.display();

}
person::person(int i, char *s)    // Constructor
{

    age = i;
    strcpy(name, s);

}
void person::display(void)
{

    cout << name << " is " << age << " years old." << endl;

}
```

The portions of this program that differ from the previous example have been highlighted. Very few changes have taken place. However, this example now has its own constructor, so the compiler does not need to generate one. The constructor has taken the place of the assign() method used in the earlier example and is prototyped in the **person** class template. Note that it declares no return type and has the same name as the class. The constructor function heading also reflects this. The following expression says that **person(int i, char *s)** is a constructor of class **person**. This means that no return value is expected.

```
person::person(int i, char *s)
```

The rest of the code within this constructor is identical to that used in the assign() method. Remember, assign() was a method and not a constructor, even though they both, eventually, accomplish the same thing from the on-screen viewpoint.

Under main(), the declaration of the two class objects must now be accompanied by constructor values.

```
person male(27, "Frank E. Jones");
person female(24, "Mary F. Grayson");
```

With each declaration, the constructor arguments must be included. These declarations were made on two source-code lines for the sake of clarity, but they could also have been written as follows.

```
person male(27, "Frank E. Jones"), female(24, "Mary F. Grayson");
```

The addition of the constructor means that any declaration of an object of class **person** must contain two parameters. To omit these values would result in an error when attempting to compile the source code.

The requirement that initialization values be provided with each object declaration can be a liability in some usages and an asset in others. However, there is a convenient way around this. Referring to an earlier discussion on default parameter values, the **person** class might be written in the following manner.

```
class person {
    private:
        int age;
        char name[50];
    public:
        person(int x = 0, char *c = ""); //Constructor
        void        display(void);
};
```

The change here involves the constructor prototype that now contains default values. These, more or less, reflect what a default constructor would do when one is not provided by the programmer. However, the programmer may wish, depending on the exact nature and needs of the object, to define some default values that have real meaning. For instance, assume that the **person** object is used for some sort of census taking. Assume also that many (but not all) of the respondents to this census whose data are to be entered are to be anonymous. With these factors in mind, the following prototype might be most appropriate.

```
person(int x = 0, char *c = "John Doe");
```

Here, the "John Doe" designation would indicate an anonymous entry. The default values can be arranged in any order to allow the object to do exactly what is required. When the constructor contains default values, declarations such as the following are perfectly legal.

```
person male, female;
```

However, this also means that it will be necessary to write another method for direct assignment.

Destructors

Just as a constructor sets aside memory space to store objects, a destructor does the reverse and releases space used for object storage. A destructor is a member function of a class and bears the same name as its class, except that a tilde (pronounced tildey) character (~) precedes this name. A class can have only one destructor, and this member function can have no arguments and can return no values. The following program is a version of the previous example that contains a constructor and a destructor.

```
#include <iostream.h>
#include <string.h>
class person {
    private:
            int age, size;
        char *name;
    public:
        person(int x = 25, int sz = 50, char *c =
"");                ~person(void);
        void display(void);
};
```

```
int main()
{

    person male(25, 15, "Frank E. Jones");
    person female(24, 16,"Mary F. Grayson");

    male.display();
    female.display();

}
person::person(int i, char *s)
{

    age = i;
    strcpy(name, s);

}
person::~person(void)
{

    delete name;

}
void person::display(void)
{

    cout << name << " is " << age << " years old." << endl;

}
```

The char array data member in the **person** class has been changed to a char pointer. A new data member named **size** has been added to the class, and the constructor has been changed to accept three values. The data member named **size** is used to indicate the string length of the person's name that will be entered. This will now be specified within the program, whereas the array provided for a 50-byte string (including the null) in the previous program example. A destructor has been added. Named **~person**, this is the same name as the class only it is preceded by the tilde. A destructor returns no value and accepts no arguments.

The code for the constructor method has been altered to reflect the changes already discussed. The value in **sz** is assigned to the **size** data member, which in turn, is used to determine the size of the memory block allocated to *****name**. The following line of code declares a **person** object named male with an **age** value of 25 and a **size** value of 15.

```
person male(25, 15, "Frank E. Jones");
```

"Frank E. Jones" contains 14 characters (including whitespaces), so 15 bytes of memory will be required to store these data (including the \0). The **size** value of 15 will be used by the **new** operator to set aside this number of bytes for storage.

The destructor contains a single statement.

```
delete name;
```

The destructor uses the delete operator to release the block of memory previously allocated to ***name** within the object. With the inclusion of this destructor, the memory block is not tied up after it is no longer needed.

A destructor is called implicitly (internally and by default) when a variable goes outside of its declared scope. Destructors for local variables are called when the block in which they are declared becomes inactive. However, when pointers to objects go out of scope, a destructor is not implicitly called. This means that the **delete** operator must be explicitly called by the programmer to destroy the object. Such is the case in the above example. The constructor allows the object to be declared with a size value. The destructor calls **delete** to destroy the object (and thus free up memory) when the object goes out of scope.

When a destructor is not defined for a class, one that does absolutely nothing is created by default. For this reason, many classes use this default destructor, as is evidenced by the absence of any destructor definition.

The creation of a constructor that initializes class objects on declaration has not entirely relieved the necessity of using an assignment method. The constructor used in the previous program example took the place of assign() but only because each class object simply received an initial assignment. No **reassignments** were necessary to the operation of this program. However, if values within a previously declared object are to be changed, then some sort of assignment method/operator is necessary.

The following program segment introduces a discussion about class data member assignment operators.

```
class person {
    private:
        int age;
        char name[50];
    public:
        person(int x = 25, char *c = "");
        void display(void);
};

int main()
{

    person male(25, "Frank E. Jones"), female;

    female = male;

    male.display();
    female.display();

}
```

This is quite similar to an earlier program example where **name** is a simple char array and not a declared char pointer. The **male** object is initialized directly while the **female** object receives the default values. However, the next line makes an assignment.

```
                female = male;
```

The code bodies of various methods (discussed previously) are not shown in this example for the sake of brevity. It is assumed that they exist in their original form. When this program is executed, it will display the following on the monitor screen.

```
        Frank E. Jones is 25 years old.
        Frank E. Jones is 25 years old.
```

This display occurs because the male and female objects are identical.

It has already been established that class objects default to private and cannot be accessed by other functions or operators that are not a part of that class. In the previous class, **age** and **name[]** are private, but it appears as though they have been accessed by the intrinsic assignment operator (=). How can this be, if they are truly private? After all, the assignment operator is intrinsic, isn't it?

The answer to this last question is, "It can be." But in this usage, the intrinsic assignment operator definitely will not work on class assignments handled in this manner. The above program has made use of a **special assignment operator method** that was not defined in the class definitions. This operator was created by default because no user-written definition was found by the compiler. The compiler detected a condition where two operands of the assignment operator were of class **person** (non-intrinsic); therefore, the derived operator was created by default. This default assignment operator caused an exact copy of right operand to be read into the left operand. This copy was made on a bit-by-bit basis.

This is a simple program example, and the default assignment operator created by the compiler for this class is adequate. However, if an attempt had been made to do the same thing with the modification of this program that declared **name** a char pointer instead of a char array, a null pointer assignment would result. This would mean that a value was assigned to a pointer that had not been initialized.

This discussion points to the fact that complex class definitions require more than the very basic assignment operator function that is generated by default. The only safe way to proceed when class assignments must be made, as in the class example where *__name__ is a char pointer, is to create an assignment operator function such as the one that follows.

```
void person::operator = (const person &wholeclass)
{

    age = wholeclass.age;
    size = wholeclass.size;
    name = new char[size];  // initialize pointer
    strcpy(name, wholeclass.name);

}
```

Operator functions have been previously discussed, so this example should not present anything radically new. The '=' operator is declared an operator function of type **person** with a void return. The argument to this operator function or method is a pointer to the **person** class. Within the method source code, the member-of operator is used to access the values. This is permitted because the operator function is of type **person**. The complete program follows.

```cpp
#include <iostream.h>
#include <string.h>
class person {
    private:
        int age, size;
        char *name;
    public:
        person(int x = 25, int size = 50, char *c = "");
        ~person(void);
        void display(void);
        void operator = (const person &perclass);
};
int main()
{

    person male(25, 15, "Frank E. Jones");
    person female;

    female = male;

    male.display();
    female.display();

}
person::person(int i, int sz, char *s)
{

    age = i;
    size = sz;
    name = new char[size];
    strcpy(name, s);

}
person::~person(void)
{

    delete name;

}
```

```
void person::display(void)
{

    cout << name << " is " << age << " years old." << endl;

}
void person::operator = (const person &wholeclass)
{

    age = wholeclass.age;
    size = wholeclass.size;
    name = new char[size];
    strcpy(name, wholeclass.name);

}
```

Certainly, a more complex class definition would require an equally complex operator function definition, but this example presents the overall concept well.

The prototype for the operator method declares that '=' is an operator method of type **person** and returns void. The argument to this operator method is the address of the class that serves as its right operand. This is a class of type **person**. If this operator method were not included, then the compiler would try to create one. The compiler-created operator method would be similar, but it would not address the char pointer assignment in the same way that this custom method does, and a null pointer assignment would be the result. It must be remembered that the compiler will attempt to create the necessary assignment operator code by default if one is not provided by the programmer. However, this is a rather primitive process, and there is no guarantee that it will succeed. Therefore, the C++ programmer should rarely (if ever) depend on the default methods in such exercises unless the class is extremely simple in content and capable of being addressed by such default constructions.

Notice that every statement in the executable portion of the program (under main()) is user-defined. Not a single intrinsic function, statement, or operator is used. The entire execution chain is carried out using the behavior of the **person** object. This is OOP!

The behavior of the **person** class is determined solely by the programmer. While the **person** class does only a few things at this point, its personality can be changed to respond to the need for that object to do more. As an example, imagine that it is necessary for the object to be able to compare the ages of the individuals whose records are contained in the **person** class. This personality trait could be accomplished by adding the following method.

```
int person::operator < (person s)
{
    if (age < s.age)
        return(-1);
    else
        return(0);
}
```

This is an operator function that uses the '<' operator (less than). Within the function body, the values in the **age** data member are compared. This operator works with objects in the same manner that it does with intrinsic data types by returning a value of zero when a FALSE condition exists and a value other than zero (−1) when a TRUE condition occurs. This function returns an int type and can be used in standard **if-else** conditional tests, as shown below.

```
class person {
    private:
        int age, size;
        char *name;
    public:
        person(int x = 25, int size = 50, char *c = "");
        ~person(void);
        void display(void);
        void operator = (const person &perclass);
        int operator < (person c);
};

int main()
{

    person male(20, 15, "Frank E. Jones");
    person female(23, 17, "Grace F. Hedrick");

    if (male < female)
        male.display();
    else
        female.display();

}
// Method code bodies are placed here
```

This program will display the following text on the monitor.

```
Frank E. Jones is 20 years old.
```

This display results because the age of the **male** object is lower than the age of the **female** object. The overloaded '<' operator is used to determine which object contains the lowest age value. However, some of the pure object-oriented approach has been lost in this program. The ability to determine low age and display is being handled with the **intrinsic** if-else construct. What is needed is more encapsulation to return to a pure object-oriented approach.

Suppose the programmer decides that the behavior of the **person** object is to be modified to allow for direct comparison of the **age** value along with the display of the low age and name. This capability can be had by writing a method that will be arbitrarily called **display_low_age()**. The code for this method appears below.

```
void person::display_low_age(person a)
{

        if (age > a.age)
        a.display();
    else
        display();

}
```

This method compares the value of data member **age** in the calling class with the value in the same data member of the class represented in the function by **a**. If the value in a.age is lower, then a.display() is called. If not, the calling class uses its own display() function to write its value to the screen. It should be remembered that two class objects are being manipulated and compared in this method, even though only one of them is named via a calling variable (a). If this method is called in the following format, then the **age** designation in the method code body would reference **male.age**, while **a.age** is referencing **female.age**.

```
male.display_low_age(female)
```

This is all that is required and leads to accomplishing the same purpose of the previous program but in a pure object-oriented manner, as is shown below.

```cpp
#include <iostream.h>
#include <string.h>
class person {
    private:
        int age, size;
        char *name;
    public:
        person(int x = 25, int size = 50, char *c = "");
        ~person(void);
        void display(void);
        void operator = (const person &perclass);
        void display_low_age(person c);
};

int main()
{

    person male(26, 15, "Frank E. Jones");
    person female(23, 17, "Grace F. Hedrick");

    male.display_low_age(female);

}
// Method code goes here
```

This would work in exactly the same manner if the call to display_low_age() had been that shown below.

```cpp
            female.display_low_age(male);
```

The same result is obtained because the display_low_age() method compares the argument class with the calling class. Either way, this program has returned to a pure object-oriented approach.

The **person** class began as an extremely simple object, but it has grown considerably as more has been added to its personality. The program below shows the entire source code as it appears to this point in the discussion.

```
#include <iostream.h>
#include <string.h>
class person {
    private:
        int age, size;
        char *name;
    public:
        person(int x = 25, int size = 50, char *c = "");
        ~person(void);
        void display(void);
        void operator = (const person &perclass);
        void display_low_age(person c);
};

int main()
{

    person male(26, 15, "Frank E. Jones");
    person female(23, 17, "Grace F. Hedrick");

    male.display_low_age(female);

}
person::person(int i, int sz, char *s)
{

    age = i;
    size = sz;
    name = new char[size];
    strcpy(name, s);

}
*person::~person(void)
{

    delete name;

}
```

```
void person::display(void)
{

    cout << name << " is " << age << " years old." << endl;

}
void person::operator = (const person &wholeclass)
{

    age = wholeclass.age;
    size = wholeclass.size;
    name = new char[size];
    strcpy(name, wholeclass.name);

}
int person::operator < (person s)
{

    if (age < s.age)
        return(-1);
    else
        return(0);
}
void person::display_low_age(person a)
{

    if (a.age < age)
        a.display();
    else
        display();

}
```

If the main() portion of the program is removed, what remains is the object structure. It has grown considerably, but this is still a very simple object. However, it is beginning to take on personality traits that are highly individualistic. It is a unique object with unique behavior and characteristics. Such is the case with all objects in OOP.

Multiple Access Specifiers

It is not unusual to encounter multiple access specifiers in class definitions. Once a specifier is used, that particular means of access remains in force, unless modified by another access specifier. While it is practical to group all data members and methods in a class according to access, it may be more expressive to group data and methods in a more logical manner, regardless of access level. The following class demonstrates this.

```
class animal {
    private:
        char *bird[60];
        char *reptile[35];
        char *mammal[45];
        char *amphib[15];
    public:
        void setbird(char *b);
        void setrep(char *r);
        void setmam(char *m);
        void setamp(char * b);
        void sortbird(void);
        void sortrep(void);
        void sortmam(void);
        void sortamp(void);



};
```

All data members are declared private, while all methods are public. All class members are grouped according to access. However, it might be more expressive to write this class in the manner shown below.

```
class animal {
    private:
        char *bird[60];
    public:
        void setbird(char *b);
        void sortbird(void);
    private:
        char *reptile[35];
    public:
        void setrep(char *r);
        void sortrep(void);
```

```
    private:
        char *mammal[45];
    public:
        void setmam(char *m);
        void sortmam(void);
    private:
        char *amphib[15];
    public:
        void setamp(char * b);
        void sortamp(void);

};
```

Both classes perform exactly the same thing. From the compiler's viewpoint, both are identical in structure. With a relatively small number of total class members, perhaps one form is just as good as another. However, the latter form may prove to be far more expressive, especially when classes with a large number of data members and methods are involved. Remember, the access specifier continues in force with regard to all class members that follow until and unless another access specifier is encountered.

As previous program examples have shown, when data members of a class are private, they may be accessed only via methods of the same class. No other means of access is possible. None of the standard C++ functions or intrinsic operators will be able to access the members of a class that are made private.

Classes and Inline Functions

Inline functions in classes are perfectly legal and highly desirable in many applications. The following program is an incomplete version of a previous example that incorporates an inline function.

```
class person {
    private:
        int age, size;
        char *name;
```

```
        public:
            person(int x = 25, int size = 50, char *c = "");
            ~person(void);
            void display(void);
            void operator = (const person &perclass);
};
inline void person::display(void)
{

    cout << name << " is " << age << " years old." << endl;

}
int main()
{
    // etc. Rest of program
```

All that is necessary is to use the **inline** keyword and to insert the source code at a point in the program prior to the first call. There are no surprises here or special methods to include an inline function as a class method.

However, there is another way of accomplishing the same thing, without using the inline keyword. *Any function that is fully defined within the class structure defaults to inline.* The example below is the modified version of the previous code fragment.

```
class person {
    private:
        int age, size;
        char *name;
    public:
        person(int x = 25, int size = 50, char *c = "");
        ~person(void);
        void display(void);
        void operator = (const person &perclass);
        void person::display(void)
        {

            cout << name << " is " << age << " years
old." << endl;

        }
};
```

Notice that the entire function body of display() appears within the class. The separate prototype is no longer necessary because the function is wholly defined within the class. Because this is an inline function (by default), a source copy of it will be made each time a class object is declared within the calling program. This accurately defines an inline function. No inline keyword is required, because this is a default condition of functions defined within a class. Following the formerly discussed rule of implementing inline functions, the function will be made inline by default only if it is possible to do so owing to memory availability. If not, it will be compiled as a standard member function (method).

It can be seen that a class is a self-contained, encapsulated bundle of an object's data structure and methods for controlling and manipulating those data. The bundling of data and methods is called *encapsulation* in object-oriented terminology.

Encapsulation is a black box method of addressing a task. The exact manner in which an operation is handled is hidden. C++ classes hide complexity by concealing internal data structures and methods and by providing programmers with a data interface that does not require knowledge of the internal working structure. Initially, this may sound strange, since it is necessary for the programmer to build these classes; which does require knowledge of the internal working structure. However, as programming assignments pile up and more and more code is written, specific knowledge of the exact code that allows these operations to take place dims in the programmer's mind. The fact that **Object A** can do a certain group of tasks is enough. It is not necessary to have continued intimate knowledge of the mechanics that allow these tasks to be accomplished.

There are many common parallels to this black box concept. Programmers deal with them every day. Consider the printf() function, for example. Few programmers are truly knowledgeable about the exact source code that goes into the printf() function. It's enough to know that it will process data in a certain manner. The programmer knows what printf() will do, even though there is no knowledge of exactly how it does it. The same can be said for most of the other functions, statements, and operators common to C++ and every other language.

When programmers begin using a language, they (unknowingly) accept the black box nature of its statements and functions. This is the starting point for addressing tasks in this language. Further in-depth knowledge of the internal architecture of the language for most of these operations is totally unnecessary. By using OOP in C++, the programmer can establish a new starting point. Through the programming objects, it might be said that the starting point in addressing a task lies in knowing what the object can do and not in how it does it.

Object Design Criteria

The first step in creating an object is to determine the exact nature of what the object is to do. Through C++ classes, the programmer defines a class type along with the behavior of this type. It can be said that the newly defined class is a derived type (derived from existing types), but this is not entirely accurate. In fact, this new object is a user-defined type as opposed to a derived type. Some experts say that a user-defined type is, of necessity, a derived type, because it stems from the tools already locked into the language. Others say that a new class is not a true derived type, because the combination presents a unique bundle, not specifically related to other types of operations. This latter group opines that *user-defined type* is the only proper designation. The argument carries over into lengthy discussions on just what is meant by OOP.

Regardless of terminology, a C++ object is defined by the user as to content and behavior. The C++ programmer must give great thought to both class content and behavior, the latter term being applied to the mechanisms that manipulate the data members.

In designing a new class, it is perhaps most helpful to begin with a brief description of behavior. For instance:

```
"A class that will sort a group of ten integers and ten doubles in
    ascending order and display these results in two columns on the
    screen."
```

```
"A class that will contain the names, addresses, length of
employment, and current salary of a group of 50 employees and
calculate withholding for each employee for each pay period."
```

```
"A class that will create a vertical and horizontally scrolled
window and write centered data in the window."
```

These simple descriptions provide the programmer with the concept behind each class object and allow for the task of actually building that object to begin. For example, the first description would most likely require data members that consist of, at minimum, an integer array and a double array, each capable of storing ten values. Add to this a method to load the values as a group or individually, a method to sort the int values and the double values. Finally, a display method that the lists into columns would be required. This information should be listed in logical order.

```
1. int array - 10 elements
2. double array - 10 elements
3. assign method
4. ascending sort method
5. column display method
```

This list can then be analyzed and will accept additions as the process continues. With these criteria in mind, a class called **sortnums** might be the final result, along with a calling sequence that might appear as follows.

```
sortnums num1;

num1.assign(i, d); // i and d are arrays of numbers
num1.sort();    // sort numbers in ascending order
num1.displaycol();// display sorted list in columns
```

It is not difficult to imagine what the coding contents of each method might be.

Most of the examples in this book deal with very simple tasks, but objects can definitely grow with the need for more capability. An object that can accomplish five different operations today might be expanded to accomplish twenty or more in the future.

Suppose it is decided that the assignment, sorting, and display methods of this class are to be combined in one operation. Then, the behavior of the class can be immediately changed. The following method might be called to load the information from the two arrays, automatically sort these values into ascending order, and display them in columns on the screen.

```
num1.do_all(x, d);
```

This combines the three discrete operations into one. The personality of the object has changed to address the task at hand. This new object is as unique as the previous one. Each exhibits a different personality.

By preparing a brief, written description of the behavior or personality of an object before the actual coding begins, the programmer should be able to work more efficiently. This method is preferred over determining class behavior while in the middle of the coding process. By gaining a clear idea of the class behavior as a whole from the start, the object may be built as a unique entity as opposed to a combination of individual components.

This process is not unlike the steps that are taken in building an ANSI C program. However, the concept is also considerably different, in that it is necessary to encapsulate all of the methods for data manipulation. The programmer must concentrate on the mini-world aspect of OOP in an attempt to provide the object with the capability of addressing all of the necessary tasks as a single unit or bundle. While this mode of thinking and planning may seem strange initially, as the beginning C++ programmer builds more classes, the process evolves into one where operations are carried out in a natural, human manner. This is really what OOP is all about.

In learning to design and work with classes in C++, it is inefficient to plunge in without some sort of design regimen in mind. This concept *map* must start with a fairly specific idea of what the object is to be. At this point, the behavior of the object is the critical factor. After listing behavioral attributes, the programmer can then approach the actual coding in a logical manner.

This approach should save many hours of time wasted fixing code when the programmer becomes lost in a maze of code brought on by ideas that he or she did not fully think out before beginning the coding. It is not unusual for objects to take on gigantic proportions, so the list of capabilities may fill many pages. However, each behavioral attribute is programmed a step at a time. The end result will be a bundle of small components that form a large, complex object, an object that is treated as a single, totally unique entity.

Summary

The discussions in this chapter have dealt with classes, the true objects in OOP using C++. Many beginning C++ programmers lean heavily on the operational relationship that C++ classes exhibit when compared with C++ enhanced structs. However, the concepts behind the two are completely different. C++ programmers will use structs almost exclusively for bundling data members. While these structs may have member functions, most programmers will not include them. Whenever programming requires the bundling of data members and member functions, the C++ class will (and should) be used exclusively.

While C++ classes have been explored in this chapter, the most important aspect of these discussions lies in explaining the object-oriented concept. This has involved the encapsulation of data and methods that result in a unique object with unique behavioral characteristics that might be better defined as the personality of the object.

Operationally, the C++ object is self-contained. It provides its own mechanisms for assignment, manipulation, creation, and destruction. This, then, satisfies the mini-world concept that lies behind the ability to address tasks in an object-oriented manner.

This chapter has taken the reader through another step in learning true OOP. At this point, programmers making the journey from C to C++ should begin to think automatically in an object-oriented manner. The object is the bundling of data members and methods contained in a class. The class is the object and it is treated as a single, unique entity, different from all others. All assignments and operations are carried out via the object, proper, as opposed to accessing discrete data within the object.

When this principle is carried over into addressing tasks, a completely new area of possibilities opens up. There still exist tasks that can be best handled through procedural-based programming, but there are many others that will best fit the object-oriented approach. By understanding both approaches, the best method of accomplishing any task may be effectively determined.

Chapter 6
++++++++++++
Inheritance

Chapter 5 introduced fairly complex object-oriented concepts. This chapter delves more deeply into classes, discussing how these objects can spawn other objects. More new concepts are presented, and the reader will become familiar with inheritance, friends, polymorphism, and other OOP principles. While these discussions may initially seem a bit foreign, they are natural extensions of what has been learned in previous chapters. Having absorbed these previous materials, the reader should have little difficulty in moving farther into the world of OOP using C++.

The discussions that follow take up where the last chapter left off and use the **person** class as a basis. The expanded person class as discussed in the last chapter is shown below.

```
#include <iostream.h>
#include <string.h>
class person {
    private:
        int age, size;
        char *name;
    public:
        person(int x = 25, int size = 50, char *c ="");
        ~person(void);
        void display(void);
        void operator = (const person &perclass);
        void display_low_age(person c);
};

int main()
{

    person male(26, 15, "Frank E. Jones");
    person female(23, 17, "Grace F. Hedrick");
```

```
        male.display_low_age(female);

}
person::person(int i, int sz, char *s)
{

    age = i;
    size = sz;
    name = new char[size];
    strcpy(name, s);

}
person::~person(void)
{

    delete name;

}
void person::display(void)
{

    cout << name << " is " << age << " years old." << endl;

}
void person::operator = (const person &wholeclass)
{

    age = wholeclass.age;
    size = wholeclass.size;
    name = new char[size];
    strcpy(name, wholeclass.name);

}
void person::display_low_age(person a)
{

    if (a.age < age)
        a.display();
    else
        display();

}
```

Treating complex data groupings as a single object offers many advantages, but it also presents some problems that must be addressed. The **display_low_age** method was incorporated to display the low age value within the person class. It accepts an argument of a person class and compares the **age** value in the argument class with the same value in the calling class.

```
void person::display_low_age(person a)
{

    if (age > a.age)
        a.display();
    else
        display();

}
```

When used in the following format where **male** and **female** are objects of type **person**, the low age value will be displayed on the monitor screen.

```
                male.display_low_age(female);
```

This method performs the task, but it does seem slightly odd in that it doesn't fit the usual format of a function or method that compares two arguments and returns or displays the lower of the two. Certainly, it does compare two values, the first within the calling object (male) and the second within the argument object (female). However, this method is a bit off beat in appearance and usage. This is not to be avoided necessarily, as it is not unusual for OOP applications to reveal a strange twist or two. However, a programmer should not purposely leave the straight and narrow without some justifiable cause for doing so.

   To address the unusual nature of the display_low_age() method, the programmer's first inclination might be to develop a comparison method that would accept two object arguments. The age values in these two objects would then be compared and the lower of the two would be displayed. It might be used in the following format.

```
display_low_age(male, female);
```

This function would accomplish the same end result, but it would do so in a more acceptable manner. However, there is a problem. If this method is a member of a class, then it must be called as such. It cannot simply be used in stand-alone fashion, assuming that the **age** element within the class is private.

Therefore, the only practical manner in which to arrive at a process that will compare the age elements of two **person** class objects without being called as a class method is to use an exterior function, one that is not a member of any class.

The easiest way to accomplish this is to write a separate function that is not a member of class **person**. However, this function must, in some manner, be given access to the private data members while not actually being a member of the same class(es). It has been firmly stated that private data members in a class can be accessed only by methods of that class *unless* special access is granted to other functions. It is in this area that the so-called friend functions become important.

Friend Functions

Fortunately, C++ was designed to allow for the granting of special access privileges to functions that are not a part of a class. This is where a **friend** or **friend function** must be utilized. The following program closely mimics the earlier example, but it operates in a more orthodox manner.

```
#include <iostream.h>
#include <string.h>
class person {
    private:
        int age, size;
        char *name;
    public:
        person(int x = 25, int size = 50, char *c ="");
        ~person(void);
        void display(void);
        void operator = (const person &perclass);
        friend void display_low_age(person a, person b);
};
```

```
int main()
{

    person male(26, 15, "Frank E. Jones");
    person female(23, 17, "Grace F. Hedrick");

    display_low_age(male, female);

}
void display_low_age(person a, person b)
{

    if (b.age > a.age)
        a.display();
    else
        b.display();

}
```

The code for the previous method bodies is purposely omitted here to save space and to highlight the changes. (If a working program is to be compiled, then this code must be included.) The major differences are highlighted in this listing and include the **friend** classification of the function within the class body, the altered call made under main(), and the body for the new function.

In this program, display_low_age() is declared a **friend** of class person. This means that the function is granted full access to all of the private members of the **person** class. Within the class definition, the display_low_age() function prototype is found. However, it should be firmly established that *display_low_age() is in no way a method (member function) of the person class*. It is a discrete function that has been granted special access to the members of this class by means of the friend declaration.

A friend function, then, is a function that is not a method of a class but that has been granted full access to the members of that class, even those that are private. Notice that the code for the friend function is very standard. There are no special designations within the code body. The only special treatment this function has received lies in its being declared a friend within the class body.

This friend function accepts two arguments, each of which must be an object of type person. It will compare the **age** member values in each class object and display the formatted contents of the object with the lowest

age value. Many programmers will be more comfortable with this manner of accomplishing the task at hand than with the class member method discussed previously.

Most functions can be made friends of any class. However, if numerous friend functions are involved in an application, the whole concept of OOP is lost. Friend functions are quite welcome on rare occasions, but they are not to be overly encouraged as their overuse can muddy and even destroy the OOP process.

In some instances, the use of a friend function is logical and warranted, but these are few and far between. OOP is an excellent method of programming, but there are times when a slight reversion toward procedural-based programming can be more practical. The friend function concept might be thought of as a *window* of procedural-based programming within a framework of OOP. Again, it should be used quite sparingly. Friend functions are used to keep class objects at minimum size as well as to enhance object performance.

There are restrictions on the types of functions that can be declared friends of a class: Constructors, destructors, assignment operator functions, class type operator functions, and virtual functions cannot be named friends.

There is no limit to the number of friend functions that a class may have. A class may even be granted friend status. When an entire class is to be made a friend of another class, it is necessary that the class that is to receive friend status be declared before the class that designates it as a friend. The code fragment that follows demonstrates this.

```
class alpha {
    //class contents

};

class beta {
    private:
        int x, y;
    public:
        beta(int i = 0, int j = 0)
        {
            x = i;
            y = j;
        }

        friend class alpha;  // declare class alpha as a friend

};
```

In this example, class alpha is designated a friend of class beta. Notice that class alpha was declared prior to class beta, which names alpha as a friend. With class alpha granted friend status of class beta, every member function of class alpha becomes a friend of class beta. When a class is made a friend, access is unimportant. Members that are private, public, or protected are completely accessible by the friend class.

No class or function can declare itself to be a friend of another class. Only the class which is to relinquish access to the friend can make this declaration. Alpha is a friend of beta, and permission was granted by class beta.

The object-oriented concept of a class is that of a collection of data that is treated as a single, unique object. Access specifiers are used within a class to limit access by entities that lie outside of the scope of that class. However, there occasionally comes a time when it is desirable to bend these rules just a bit to take care of a particular programming task. The friend concept allows for this while it maintains the integrity of the class in regard to access attempts from entities outside of the scope.

Inheritance Principles

Past examples of class usage have involved only single classes—that is, one class that is enclosed and not related in any manner to another class. Individual classes contain their own members and methods, and these are totally unrelated to any other class members. However, the object-oriented power of C++ lies in its ability to spawn other classes from a root or base class. This process is called **inheritance** and is a concept whereby one class may receive methods and members from another class. The class that inherits is called the **derived** class, while the class inherited from is the **base** class.

OOP is heavily involved in data encapsulation, and every program statement can be made an encapsulated part of a single class. This has been done in the most recent program examples. However, many programming tasks are best addressed by incorporating multiple classes, resulting in a number of encapsulations. Out of coding necessity, it may be essential that these block objects have some relationship with each other.

Relating this process to the real world, the topic of automobiles makes a convenient reference. The base class might be called TRANSPORTATION, and it could include members that address the ability to move and to contain a payload. From this class, two other classes, one named TRUCK, the other named CAR, might be derived. From each of these classes, two other classes might be derived, named DRIVE_TRAIN and BODY_STYLE, respectively. This expansion can continue to pyramid. The following chart shows the breakdown to this point.

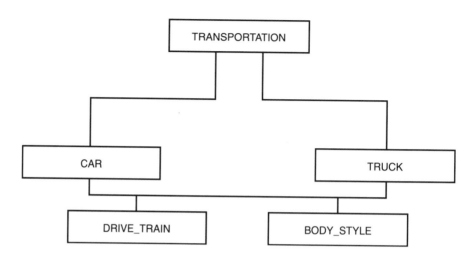

Each of the blocks in the diagram represents a different class; however, each is derived from the base class named TRANSPORTATION. The encapsulation used here is not total because a single class does not contain all of the complex object characteristics. In real-world examples, it is necessary to differentiate, and object-oriented programs that address such real-world objects must do likewise.

It is necessary in the real world to differentiate between a car and a truck, although both come under the general heading of transportation. The class structure above mimics this thinking process. Readers looking at the diagram can see that the inheritance involved is real. Each object derived from transportation inherits some or all of the characteristics of the class(es) that precedes it.

Through inheritance, each class object is unique but contains characteristics from the base class that are an integral part of its personality profile. In simpler terms, a human child is a unique object, but he or she inherits characteristics from the parents and could not have been created as this unique object without the parents. The same relationship can be applied to class inheritance in OOP.

To begin a practical discussion of class inheritance, let's use a program example from Chapter 4.

```
#include <iostream.h>
#include <string.h>
class person {
    private:
        int age;
        char name[50];
    public:
        person(int x, char *c); //Constructor Prototype
        void display(void);
};

int main()
{

    person male(27, "Frank E. Jones");
    person female(24, "Mary F. Grayson");

    male.display();
    female.display();

}
person::person(int i, char *s)    // Constructor
{

    age = i;
    strcpy(name, s);

}
void person::display(void)
{

    cout << name << " is " << age << " years old." << endl;

}
```

In this listing, the **person** class has been diminished somewhat from the expansions that took place in the last chapter for the sake of simplicity in moving farther into the subject of class inheritance.

In this example, class **person** contains the **name[]** array and the **age** variable. These elements are declared private. Two methods are contained in this class. Declared public, they are the **person** constructor and the display() member function. This program uses the constructor to assign the data elements and the display() method to write this information to the screen. The discussions that follow will use the **person** class as the base class. Further examples will eliminate the source code for the constructor and the display() method, again for the sake of clarity. However, the presence of this necessary code should be assumed.

The code fragment that follows again uses the **person** class template along with a new class named **record**.

```
#include <iostream.h>
#include <string.h>
class person {      // Person Class
    private:
        int age;
        char name[50];
    public:
        person(int x, char *c); // Constructor Prototype
        void display(void);

};

class record {    // record class
    private:
        int emp_years;
        double salary;
    public:
        record(int x, double d)    // Constructor
        {
            emp_years = x;
            salary = d;
        }
        void display(void) // display method
        {
            cout << "employed for " << emp_years << " years
at a salary of $" << salary << endl;

        }

};
```

At this point, there is absolutely no relationship between the **person** class and the **record** class. We can see that the record class has its own constructor and a display() method that writes information to the screen. Even though this method has the same name as a similar method within the **person** class, they are unrelated. Using these two classes, the following program might be displayed.

```
// Class definitions are included here
int main()
{

    person male(27, "Frank E. Jones");
    record emp(4, 435.50);

    male.display();
    emp.display();

}
```

Again for the sake of simplicity, the actual class declarations are not contained in this code example. Simply assume that they are present. As stated earlier, these two classes (**person** and **record**) have no connection with each other at this point. Within the above code listing, **male** becomes an object of type **person** and **emp** an object of type **record**. Each is initialized upon declaration. Next, the loaded data are displayed using the discrete display() methods of each class. The end result is the following display.

```
Frank E. Jones is 27 years old
employed for 4 years at salary of $435.5
```

In combination, these two classes make some sense. For example, the **person** class contains name and age data, while the record class contains employment tenure and salary data. Since the personality of each class is so small, it would make sense from a practical standpoint to combine all the data elements into one class, assuming these data are to be connective in some manner. Imagine, however, that each class is extremely complex, containing far more data elements and methods than these simplistic examples exhibit. Assume also that the personality of each class is such that either could be used effectively in a stand-alone fashion. With this in mind, it is apparent that combining the personalities of both classes would result in a useful entity but might destroy the separate operations to which each could be applied.

To preserve the individuality of class objects, some means of separation is mandatory. However, C++ allows the programmer also to combine object personalities through inheritance while maintaining the separation. The following class structures do just this.

```
#include <iostream.h>
#include <string.h>
class person {      // Person Class
    private:
        int age;
        char name[50];
    public:
        person(int x, char *c); // Constructor Prototype
        void display(void);

};


class record : public person {    // record class derived from person class
    private:
        int emp_years;
        double salary;
    public:
        record(int xx, char *cc, int i, double d) : person(xx, cc)    //  New Constructor
        {
            emp_years = i;
            salary = d;
        }
        void display(void) // New display method
        {

            person :: display();
            cout << "employed for " << emp_years << " years at a salary of $" <<
salary << endl;


        }

};
```

Examine the declaration of the **record** class in the example above.

```
class record : public person
```

This expression states that the **record** class is derived from the **person** class. The public access specifier is used to make this declaration. This means that the public members of the base class (person) are now public members of the derived class (record). However, the private members of the base class are still private, and the derived class has no direct access to them.

In the current example, the constructor and the display() method within the **person** class are now an official part of the **record** class. Other modes of a derived class object are protected and private, which will be discussed later.

This entire derivation process has gained a great deal of versatility for the programmer. The **record** class has been greatly expanded. Its personality has been changed to a combination of what it was before and what was offered by the **person** class. However, the **person** class is totally unchanged. It may be used exactly as it was prior to this inheritance procedure. The person class becomes a part of the derived class but still remains a separate, usable entity.

Of prime importance is the fact that the constructor and the display() method in the record class have also been changed in order to mate with the person class. Due to using the public access specifier in declaring that **record** is derived from **person**, only the public elements of the base class (person) are directly available to the **record** class. Therefore, the **record** class cannot contain its own methods to address the two data elements in **person**. However, the **person** constructor and the **person display()** method are available to **record**, since they were among the public entities of the base class. Since these two methods are available to the derived class, they can be used by **record** to assign and display the contents of the private data elements in **person**. This is not a direct access procedure, since the **record** class must use the base class public methods to accomplish these operations.

A new constructor has been used with the record class. The source code for this method is shown below.

```
record(int xx, char *cc, int i, double d) : person(xx, cc)
{
    emp_years = i;
    salary = d;
}
```

This constructor has been modified to include the **person** class constructor. Now, declaring an object of **record** class will involve four initialization values. These are represented in the method header by the following parameters.

```
int xx, char *cc, int i, double d
```

Shown below is the expression that follows this opening segment of the constructor.

```
: person(xx, cc)
```

This means that the first two values handed to the **record** constructor will serve as arguments to the **person** constructor. Bear in mind that the **record** class does not have direct access to the private data members of the **person** class. Therefore, a method cannot be written for the **record** class that directly addresses the **age** and **name[]** data members. However, the **record** class does have access to the **person** constructor that can access these data members. By going through the **person** constructor, indirect access is gained. The **record** constructor can now be used to assign values to the private data members of the **record** class and through the **person** constructor to initialize the private members of the base class.

The code for the **record** object display() method is shown below.

```
void display(void) // New display method
{

    person :: display();
    cout << "employed for " << emp_years << " years at a salary of $"
<< salary << endl;

}

};
```

This method has been altered also to call the display() method within the **person** class. The scope resolution operator (::) is necessary for this call. The new **record** display() method now calls the **person** display() method before executing the remainder of its code body.

The **record** class has a brand new personality that is used in a different and expanded manner than its previous personality, but the base class, **person**, is totally unchanged. It may still be used for the purposes outlined in the last chapter.

Summarizing this procedure of inheritance, the **record** class is derived from the **person** class. This latter entity is now known as the base class. Do not be confused into thinking that the **person** class can be individually initialized with useful information that can then be sampled from the **record** class. This is not the case. The public portions of the **person** class template are now a direct part of the **record** class through inheritance. The private data members of this template are not directly available but can be accessed indirectly through the public member functions that are a part of the **person** class and that have been inherited by **record**. This expansion of the **record** class has involved another class template. However, the **record** class is a unique entity because of this inheritance. It exhibits traits of the **person** class, but it is unique in its overall personality.

The following program shows how the **record** class might now be utilized.

```
// person and record class code is located here

int main()
{

    record emp(27, "Frank E. Jones", 4, 435.5);
    emp.display();

}
```

An object of type **person** is not found in the program. The only object is of type **record**. The (discrete) **person** class is simply not used. The **person** class template, however, is utilized from within the **record** class through its inheritance.

The examples discussed in these pages are very basic and simple. To get the full impact of inheritance and the advantages it offers, it is necessary to imagine a typical class construct that may have hundreds or even thousands of code lines. From a base class construct, new classes may be constructed without repeating necessary source code. This is done through inheritance. By properly utilizing the C++ class inheritance capabilities, all or a portion of one class may serve as a part of the personality of another class.

It is most important to realize that constructors and destructors of the base class are not inherited by the derived class. Therefore, the constructor for the derived **record** class requires parameter information for the constructor of the base (**person**) class.

In the current code example, the base class constructor is called by **person(xx, cc)**. Here, **person** is the constructor name, while **xx** and **cc** are part of its parameter list. These examples do not include destructors at this time. (This subject will be discussed in Chapter 6.) Therefore, default destructors are automatically generated. These are adequate for the specific examples discussed in this chapter. However, more complex classes require an explicit (programmer-written) destructor. Since destructors are not inherited by derived classes, it is necessary to carry the destruction process down through the class hierarchy, ending with the base class.

The overloaded **record** display() method calls the **person** display() method, which it may access because of the derivation. It then incorporates its own call to the C++ iostream to write the values in **i** and **d** to the screen.

It is necessary to call the **person** display() function because this is the only function that can display the values of the private data members in the **person** class. A publicly derived class cannot access the private members of the base class. This restriction prevents a derived class from overriding the privacy control of the base class. All public members (data, method, etc.) are accessible by the derived class, but that is not the case in the program example under discussion. Here, the data members of the **person** base class are private.

Access to members of a class is controlled by the public, private, and protected access specifiers. When a derived class declares its base class public, all public members of the base class become public members of the derived class. For this reason, the **person** class constructor and the **person** class display() method become public members of the derived **record** class.

Inheritance is a one-way street. While **record** inherits from **person**, **person** does not inherit anything from **record**. With this in mind, *inheritance* is an appropriate term for what actually takes place. Inheritance is something that is passed on, nothing is passed back.

Derived Class Access

Inheritance used the public access specifier that granted the derived class access to all public elements of the base class. Used in this context,

the specifier declares the base class to be public. The private and protected access specifiers may also be used when one class is to be derived
from another.

When the base class is declared protected, the public members of the
base class become protected members of the derived class. Furthermore,
the protected members of the base class become the private members of
the derived class. All private members of the base class remain private
and are not directly accessible to the derived class.

When the base class is declared private, both protected and public
members of the base class become private members of the derived class.
As before, all private members of the base class remain private and cannot be directly accessed.

When the base class is declared public, public members of the base
class also become public members of the derived class, as demonstrated
in the earlier examples of inheritance. However, protected members of
the base class also become protected members of the derived class, while
the private base class members remain inaccessible.

In every case, the private members of the base class remain private.
There is no method whereby the private members of a base class can be
opened for outside access, other than by changing the access specifier
within the base class to public or protected.

Protected Access

Throughout previous discussions and examples, public and private access
specifiers have been used in abundance. However, the protected access
specifier has been mentioned only briefly. At this point in the journey
from C to C++, the protected specifier becomes most important.

Class members that are declared private cannot be accessed outside
of the scope of the class. Therefore, derived classes cannot use the private class members directly. Public members can be accessed from any
scope. The protected access specifier is used to provide additional programming flexibility in C++. Protected members may be accessed from
within the base class or from within any derived class providing that the
base class is declared either private or protected.

Multiple Inheritance

In the previous program example, only two classes were involved, the
base class and the single derived class. However, multiple inheritance is
allowed in C++, and it would be quite easy to include an additional class

that is derived from **record**, which in turn, is derived from **person**. If the base class (**person**) is declared public in the record class definition, the public members of **person** become public members of **record**, and these also become public members of any class derived from **record**. However, if the base class is declared private, then the third class does not inherit any of the members of the **person** base class.

The program that follows is an expanded version of an earlier example. Class **person** is the base class, while **record** is derived from **person** and class **pension** is derived from **record**. The previous contents of the **person** and **record** classes are assumed to make this example as simple as possible.

```
class person {
    // class contents
};

class record : public person {
    // class contents
};

class pension : public record {  // pension class derived from
record
    private:
        int retire_year;
        double monthly_pension;
    public:
        pension(int x, char *c, int i, double d, int ry, double
mp) : record(x, c, i, d)
    {
        retire_year = ry;
        monthly_pension = mp;
    }
    void display(void)  // New display method
    {

        record :: display();
        cout << "Retirement year is 19" << retire_year << " at a
monthly rate of " << "$" << monthly_pension << endl;

    }

};
```

```
int main()
{

    pension emp(27, "Frank E. Jones", 4, 435.50, 98, 775.15);

    emp.display();

}

// Code body for methods appears here
```

This program will display the following.

```
Frank E. Jones is 27 years old
employed for 4 years at a salary of $435.5
Retirement year is 1998 at a monthly rate of $775.15
```

Each line of this display example denotes a different class template and shows a clear picture of the inheritance that has taken place beginning with the **person** base class.

The inheritance is straightforward. The new **pension** class inherits all of the public member functions (methods) from both **person** (the base class) and **record**. The **pension** class does not have direct access to any of the private members of **record** or **person**. However, these members may be indirectly accessed via their respective constructors.

The constructor used in the **pension** class references the constructor from the **record** class. It, in turn, has used the constructor from the base class. The display() method used within the **pension** class calls the display method from the **record** class as well.

As stated earlier in this chapter, the class examples used in this discussion are extremely simple to gain the best instructive advantage. Even with this simplicity, the total class hierarchy has grown to appreciable size, as demonstrated by the full source code shown below.

```
#include <iostream.h>
#include <string.h>
class person {      // Person Class
    private:
        int age;
        char name[50];
```

```
    public:
        person(int x, char *c); // Constructor Prototype
        void display(void);

};

class record : public person {   // record class derived from
person class
    private:
        int emp_years;
        double salary;
    public:
        record(int x, char *c, int i, double d) : person(x, c)
//   New Constructor
        {
            emp_years = i;
            salary = d;
                }
        void display(void)  // New display method
        {

            person :: display();
            cout << "employed for " << emp_years << " years at a
salary of $" << salary << endl;

        }

};
class pension : public record {  // pension class derived from
record
    private:
        int retire_year;
        double monthly_pension;
    public:
        pension(int x, char *c, int i, double d, int ry, double
mp) : record(x, c, i, d)
        {
            retire_year = ry;
            monthly_pension = mp;
        }
        void display(void)  // New display method
        {

            record :: display();
```

```
        cout << "Retirement year is 19" << retire_year << " at
a monthly rate of " << "$" << monthly_pension << endl;


    }

};

int main()
{

    pension emp(27, "Frank E. Jones", 4, 435.50, 98, 775.15);

    emp.display();

}
person::person(int i, char *s)     // Constructor
{

    age = i;
    strcpy(name, s);

}
void person::display(void)
{

    cout << name << " is " << age << " years old." << endl;

}
```

Looking at the size of the source code in such a simple example, readers can easily realize that a practical example, one that accomplishes a given set of useful tasks, could be huge in comparison.

Through inheritance, the programming task can be greatly reduced by allowing base classes to spawn other classes and they, in turn, to spawn still more. Inheritance in no way changes the operation or personality of a class from which another is derived. The derived class is born with some or all of the personality of the classes from which it is derived. From there, more is added and the end result is a new personality.

Inheritance is essential to OOP and must be fully understood before programmers proceed with other processes that make this type of programming a powerful tool. Constructors and destructors of the base class are not inherited by the derived class. Therefore, the constructor for the derived class requires parameter information for the constructor of the base class. Through inheritance, base classes are able to spawn derived classes, and this is where complexities creep into object-oriented programs. However, each of these derived classes can be directly referenced to their bases. Therefore, debugging on a unit-by-unit basis is simplified.

At this point, the complex subject of inheritance has been presented using a single base class. However, it is also possible for a class to be derived from two or more base classes. Chapter 6 will delve more deeply into inheritance from multiple bases.

Polymorphism

Having laid a foundation with the discussions on class inheritance and the various modes of access, it is appropriate to move on to the more difficult subject of polymorphism. Polymorphism is defined as giving an action one name or symbol that is shared up and down a class hierarchy, with each class in the hierarchy implementing the action in a manner that is appropriate to itself. However, this definition may mean little to the reader at this juncture. The following discussions should make it clear.

Polymorphism is known also as *late binding* or *dynamic binding*. In C++, this action is accomplished in a manner where the type of an object is unidentified until run time. Polymorphism in C++ requires the use of virtual functions, which are declared with the virtual keyword. Words are not really adequate to describe polymorphism. Source code examples must be used to demonstrate this action. It should then become quite clear to the reader. Look at the following program example.

```
#include <iostream.h>
class base {
    private:
        int x, y;
    public:
        base(int i, int j)
        {

            x = i;
            y = j;

        }
```

```
            void display(void)
            {

                cout << x << " " << y << endl;

            }
};
class derived : public base {
    private:
        double d, e;
    public:
        derived(int i, int j, double a, double b) : base(i, j)
        {

            d = a;
            e = b;

        }
        void display(void)
        {

            cout << d << " " << e << " ";
            base :: display();

        }
};

int main()
{
    base alpha(44, 288);
    derived beta(22, 7, 1.5, 253.44);

    alpha.display();
    beta.display();

}
```

This is a highly simplified program that uses a base class and a derived class. For the sake of clarity, the base class is named **base** and the derived class is named **derived**. Each of these classes contains a constructor and a display() method. There is nothing unusual about either of these classes in relation to the materials already presented. The derived class utilizes the constructor and the display() method of the base class in arriving at its own constructor and display method.

Under main(), **alpha** is the base object and **beta** is the derived object. The member-of operator is used to call the display() method for each class object. This program will display the following lines on the monitor screen.

```
44 288
1.5 253.44 22 7
```

Using polymorphism, this same program can be written in a slightly different manner. Again, polymorphism is defined as giving an action one name or symbol that is shared up and down a class hierarchy, with each class in the hierarchy implementing the action in a manner that is appropriate to itself. The class hierarchy in this example is shown in block diagram form below.

This is a simple hierarchy, but it serves well as an environment in

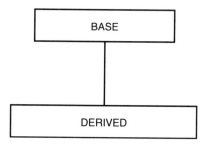

which to introduce the concept of polymorphism.

In this program example, each class has its own display method, and each display method contains the same header as shown below.

```
void display(void)
```

Each method returns a void type and accepts no arguments. Such a method makes an excellent subject to test the principles of polymorphism. The following program performs in exactly the same manner as the previous example, but it uses polymorphism in regard to the display() method.

```
#include <iostream.h>
class base {
    private:
        int x, y;
    public:
        base(int i, int j)
        {

            x = i;
            y = j;

        }
        virtual void display(void)
        {

            cout << x << " " << y << endl;

        }
};
class derived : public base {
    private:
        double d, e;
    public:
        derived(int i, int j, double a, double b) : base(i, j)
        {

            d = a;
            e = b;

        }
        virtual void display(void)
        {

            cout << d << " " << e << " ";
            base :: display();

        }
};
```

```
int main()
{
    base alpha(44, 288), *ptr;
    derived beta(22, 7, 1.5, 253.44);

    ptr = &alpha;
    ptr->display();

    ptr = &beta;
    ptr->display();

}
```

Here, base::display has been declared a virtual method. Within the body of main(), a pointer of type **base** is used to access the correct display() method. This means that the object type is not identified until run time. All invocation of display() is accomplished through the base class pointer.

A pointer (ptr) of type **base** is used for all invocations of display(). The assignment ptr = &alpha assigns the address of alpha to the base class pointer. The expression ptr->display() accesses the base::display() method by means of the base class pointer. The assignment ptr = &beta hands the address of beta to the base class pointer. The expression ptr->display() now invokes derived::display(). Any invocation of any of the display() methods is always made via the base class pointer.

Polymorphism is achieved in C++ programming with virtual member functions. However, virtual function definitions between base and derived classes must be identical. For this reason, the display() function in **derived** could not be changed as shown below.

```
virtual int display(void);
```

The definitions must be the same, which means return type and argument parameters must match. When declared virtual function definitions are different, they are *not* virtual functions. The virtual keyword is simply ignored by the compiler.

In the last program example, the display() prototype in both the base and the derived classes used the virtual keyword. Because a virtual function relies on the original class for which it is called, it is not necessary to use the virtual keyword outside of the base class. The following prototype found in the **derived** class is redundant in its use of the virtual keyword.

```
virtual void display();
```

Within the derived class, virtual could be omitted entirely, and display()
would still be a virtual function.

Polymorphism is not terribly hard to explain through examples such
as these, but demonstrating a practical use for this programming form
is more difficult. The previous example has merely shown that the dis-
play() methods are invoked at run time via the base class pointer referencing the different class objects. The following example explores some
practical uses for polymorphism.

```
#include <iostream.h>

class pet {
    private:
        char *name[3];
    public:
        pet(char *a, char *b, char *c)
        {

            name[0] = a;
            name[1] = b;
            name[2] = c;

        }
        virtual void display(void)
        {

            cout << name[0] << " " << name[1] << " " << name[2] << endl;

        }
};

class pet_order {
    private:
        pet *s[3];
    public:
        pet_order(pet *n0, pet *n1, pet *n2)
        {

            s[0] = n0;
            s[1] = n1;
            s[2] = n2;

        }
        void list(void)
```

```
            {

                int x;
                for (x = 0; x < 3; ++x)
                    s[x]->display();


            }

};
int main()
{

    pet cat("Frisky", "Puff", "Kitty");
    pet dog("Fido", "Spot", "Ruff");
    pet parakeet("Beaker", "Bluewing", "Polly");

    pet_order show(&parakeet, &dog, &cat);

    show.list();

}
```

When executed, this program will display the following lines.

```
            Beaker Bluewing Polly
            Fido Spot Ruff
            Frisky Puff Kitty
```

Two classes are used in this program, neither of which is derived from the other. The animal class contains an array of char pointers that are to be used (supposedly) to reference the names of three animals. The display() method in this class writes the names to the monitor.

The second class (**pet_order**) is used specifically for displaying pet names on the monitor in a specific order. The data member of this class is an array of pointers of type **pet**. The order in which the pet objects are given to this class constructor determines the order in which they will be displayed on the screen.

The list() method that is a part of the pet_order class references the proper object via a pointer. This is not true polymorphism, because the same display() method is used on each pass of the loop. All that is being referenced by the pointer s[x] is the specific object of type **pet**.

This works well and avoids the programmer overhead that would be necessary if each object were referenced directly as shown below.

```
parakeet.display();
dog.display();
cat.display();
```

Notice that the order in which the pointer arguments are provided to the pet_order constructor during the declaration under main() determines the order of display.

Now, assume that another class is to be added to this program, a class that will contain the names of human beings. Assume also that several **human** objects are to contain names in the same fashion as with pet objects and that these human names are to be displayed in various orders, again just like the pet names.

As shown, it would be necessary to construct a **human** class and another class called **human_order** to display the names in the same fashion. This is wasteful, since the same code would be replicated for both of the additional classes. Basically, these new additions would consist of very similar code with the class names being the only major difference. Taking this a step farther, assume that the program is to be expanded to include separate classes for draft animals, reptiles, etc. The programming overhead becomes quite sizable, and it is mandatory to attempt to share code wherever possible.

Through polymorphism, the necessity of constantly recreating the same code can be avoided entirely. The following program uses polymorphism to utilize a single show() method for displaying various lists of pet and human names.

```
#include <iostream.h>
class mammal_names {
    private:
        char *category;
    public:
        mammal_names(char *a)
        {

            category = a;

        }
```

```
            virtual void display(void)
            {

                cout << category;

            }
};

class human : public mammal_names {
    private:
        char *name[4];
    public:
        human(char *cl, char *a, char *b, char *c, char *d) : mammal_names(cl)
        {

            name[0] = a;
            name[1] = b;
            name[2] = c;
            name[3] = d;

        }
        virtual void display(void)
        {

            mammal_names::display();
            cout << ":" << name[0] << " " << name[1] << " " << name[2] <<
" " << name[3] << endl;

        }

};

class pet : public mammal_names {
    private:
        char *name[3];
    public:
        pet(char *cl, char *a, char *b, char *c) : mammal_names(cl)
        {

            name[0] = a;
            name[1] = b;
            name[2] = c;

        }
        virtual void display(void)
```

```
            {

                mammal_names::display();
                cout << ":" << name[0] << " " << name[1] << " " << name[2] << endl;

            }
};

class order {
    private:
        mammal_names *s[3];
    public:
        order(mammal_names *n0, mammal_names *n1, mammal_names *n2)
        {

            s[0] = n0;
            s[1] = n1;
            s[2] = n2;

        }
        void list(void)
        {

            int x;
            for (x = 0; x < 3; ++x)
                s[x] -> display();

        }

};
int main()
{
    mammal_names *ptr1, *ptr2, *ptr3;
    pet cat("Felines", "Frisky", "Puff", "Kitty");
    pet dog("Canines", "Fido", "Spot", "Ruff");
    human secretary("Women", "Hilda", "Pat", "Mary", "Harriet");

    ptr1 = &dog;
    ptr2 = &secretary;
    ptr3 = &cat;

    order show(ptr2, ptr3, ptr1);
    show.list();

}
```

This program won't seem so complex if it is broken down into classes and each is studied on an individual basis. Here, a base class named **mammal_names** has been created. This is a simple class that contains a single char pointer (category) as its data member, a constructor, and a display() method that is declared virtual. This method writes the object referenced by *category to the monitor.

The next class is named **human**, and it is derived from the base class. Its contents are almost identical to the **pet** class discussed earlier, only its data member is an array of four pointers (instead of three). The constructor and the display() method take this into account. The display() method references the mammal_names display() method via the scope resolution operator followed by a standard write to the iostream of the contents referenced by its array of pointers.

The **pet** class is also derived from the base class. Therefore, **pet** and **human** have the same root class but are not derived from each other in any way. The pet class remains mostly unchanged from the earlier example, although its constructor addresses the derivation, and the display() method calls the base class display() method.

The last class is named **order**, and it is identical to the pet_order class from the previous example, with the exception that the array of pointers that is its sole data member is now of type mammal_names, the base class for pet and human. Note that class **order** is not derived from any other class.

This simple rewrite of the **order** class now allows it to be used with pointers of type mammal_names. Therefore, any display() method in any class that is derived from this base class can be accommodated by the **order** list() method, as long as the display() method is virtual (i.e., contains the same return type and argument parameters of the base display() method).

Within the program portion under main(), three pointers of type mammal_names are declared. Two objects of type **pet** are declared and initialized with names. One object of type **human** is declared and initialized. Next, each pointer is assigned the address of one of the objects. Following this operation, an object named **show** (of type **order**) is declared and initialized with the pointers arranged in the desired order. When show.list() is executed, the appropriate display() methods within the complex class hierarchy are called in order.

This program will display

```
Women:Hilda Pat Mary Harriet
Felines:Frisky Puff Kitty
Canines:Fido Spot Ruff
```

Without polymorphism, it would be necessary to construct separate **order** classes for each of the name classes in order to proceed in the same programming manner. Through polymorphism, code has been shared by referencing the display() methods throughout the class hierarchy via base class pointers.

Now that this mechanism is in place, adding another class or even an additional one hundred classes is greatly simplified. The list() method in **order** simply requires a pointer of type mammal_names. Any class derived from this base class and that contains a method named display() that returns void and accepts no arguments can be referenced from within the list() method.

Polymorphism is a concept that many programmers have difficulty understanding initially. However, it is nothing more than giving an action one name that is shared over an entire class hierarchy from the base class up through the derived classes. The base and each derived class will implement this action in an appropriate manner. All of this takes place within the sample program.

Polymorphism is achieved through the use of virtual functions. The definitions of these must be identical between base and derived classes. Should there be a difference in definitions, the functions are not virtual, even though they may have been declared as such.

The great advantage gained with polymorphism is called *code-sharing*, wherein a single class or method may call up the appropriate method or methods from other classes. This saves many hours of repetitive programming. The C++ programmer must be constantly on the lookout for scenarios that lend themselves readily to a polymorphic approach.

Summary

This chapter has concentrated on the most complex aspects of OOP in C++. Through inheritance, a class may be derived from one or several other classes. A class may also be derived from a class that is itself derived from other classes. Derived classes are automatically granted access to the public members of the base class. A derived class never has access to the private members of the base class but is given access to protected members of the base class.

For derived classes, protected base class members are treated as public. However, they are not truly public, as only derived classes may have access to protected base class members. Other non-derived scopes may not access protected members of a class.

Polymorphism was also explained in considerable detail. This is a more difficult concept to grasp because a name or symbol is shared within a hierarchy (both up and down). It is not accessible outside of this hierarchy. The power behind polymorphism lies in its ability to share code or methods that act in a similar manner. Without polymorphism, object-oriented programs would quickly become unwieldy because of the programming overhead involved in constantly rewriting identical code segments.

As the programmer's experience in writing object-oriented programs increases, he or she will find ways to apply these concepts to actual programming tasks. This will require a conscious effort at first. However, as these practices become more familiar, these principles will be incorporated automatically.

Chapter 7
++++++++++++++
Addressing Real-World Tasks in an Object-Oriented Manner

The first part of this chapter expands on subject matter covered in the last chapter, with an emphasis on the methodology used to address tasks within a C++ environment. The discussion of C++ classes continues with how they may be structured and especially how they interact via inheritance. As important, these materials delve into some of the ambiguities of class inheritance.

This will be followed by discussions that take real-world events and emphasize how they may be addressed via OOP. This, then, is the methodology by which the C++ programmer may proceed to address the many complex tasks that lend themselves to OOP.

As OOP proficiency in C++ increases, programmers will find that some classes inherit from more than one base class. In such cases, the derived class inherits from multiple base classes in the same manner that previous examples inherited methods and/or access to data members from a single base class.

Unfortunately, when discussions involve multiple classes with varied inheritance paths, the program source code takes on a complexity that does not lend itself well to a popular discussion. Even though C++ has the capability of building class upon class ad infinitum, most programmers begin to get bogged down when class inheritance passes through a level of three or four hierarchies. From a practical standpoint, most tasks can be addressed by a number of discrete classes with relatively small hierarchies, even though it might be possible to combine all of the classes required into one hierarchy. Therefore, instead of addressing a specific task with a single hierarchy of sixteen classes, each of which inherits from the former, it might be addressed by eight different class hierarchies, each of which inherits from two base classes, for example.

The following program involves a single derived class that inherits from two base classes.

```
#include <iostream.h>
#include <string.h>
class base_1 {
    protected:
        int x, y;
    public:
        base_1(int i, int j)
        {
            x = i;
            y = j;
        }
        // Various methods

};

class base_2 {
    protected:
        char *a, *b;
    public:
        base_2(char *d, char *e)
        {

            a = new char[50];
            b = new char[50];

            strcpy(a, d);
            strcpy(b, e);

        }
        ~base_2(void)
        {

            delete a;
            delete b;

        }
        // Various methods

};
class derived : public base_1, public base_2 {
    private:
        char *name;
    public:
        derived (char *str, char *aa, char *bb, int xx, int
yy) : base_1(xx, yy), base_2(aa, bb){
```

```
            name = new char[50];
            strcpy(name, str);

        }
        ~derived(void)
        {

            delete name;

        }
        void display(void)
        {

            cout << name << " " << base_1::x << base_2::a <<
base_1::y << base_2::b << endl;

        }

};

int main()
{

    derived var("Numbers = ", "-fifty three   ", "-one-
hundred-ninety-eight", 53, 198);

    var.display();

}
```

The portions of the program containing parts that are new are highlighted. The class that has been named **derived** contains two base
classes, named **base_1** and **base_2**. The class definition for **derived**
names the multibase inheritance via the following code line.

```
        class derived : public base_1, public base_2
```

This states that **derived** is a class that has base_1 and base_2 as its multiple base classes. Each of the base classes is named public, although they
could also be named private or protected or even mixed with, for instance
one private and the other public.

The constructor for the derived class accesses the constructors of the two base classes using the following code.

```
derived (char *str, char *aa, char *bb, int xx, int yy) : base_1(xx, yy), base_2(aa, bb)
```

This code follows a familiar pattern except that the constructors from the two base classes are separated by a comma like the derived class definition line just discussed.

While this example will not expand further on the number of base classes, C++ certainly offers the opportunity for a class to be derived from any number of base classes. However, this will be seen rarely in most practical examples. As mentioned previously, keeping track of more than three levels of inheritance is extremely difficult, and the difficulty would apply equally to derived classes with an inordinate number of multiple base classes.

The code for the display() method is shown below.

```
cout << name << " " << base_1::x << base_2::a << base_1::y << base_2::b << endl;
```

This is handled differently from the previous examples that called display() methods from base classes. Here, the data members of the two base classes are accessed directly. This is possible because the base class data members were declared protected instead of private. Remember that protected members of a base class that is named public become **protected** members of the derived class. Therefore, all data members of the two base classes are protected members of the derived class. This means that all data members in this hierarchy are directly accessible by the derived class without having to go the indirect route via base class constructors.

The display() method that is a part of the derived class accesses directly the data members of the two base classes via the class name and the scope resolution operator. For instance, the following construct accesses the data member named **a** within the base_2 class.

```
base_2::a
```

While this program example does not provide the source code for any display() methods associated with the base classes, they certainly could be utilized in the standard fashion if they did exist.

The derived class constructor has referenced the constructors from the two base classes, but this was not mandatory. Since the derived class has complete access (protected) to the data members of both base classes, the derived class constructor could have been written by directly accessing each data member in each of the two base classes. However, since constructors were already available, it would not have made sense to go the direct-access route, as this would simply be a repetition of source code.

There are several reasons why a class might be derived from multiple base classes. All of these encompass one major concept: to better emulate real-world events. The block diagram below shows a typical example.

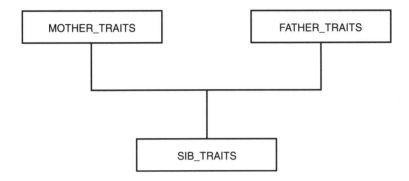

In this diagram, the SIB_TRAITS (sibling traits) class is derived from the MOTHER_TRAITS and FATHER_TRAITS classes.

The traits of the mother and the traits of the father are not related. However, the culmination of their traits are evident in the offspring. Here is a logical, real-world scenario that lends itself well to a two-based C++ inheritance hierarchy.

If this example were taken into another generation to include a grand-child, the complexity of the class hierarchy through multiple inheritance would be greatly increased, as is shown in the following block diagram.

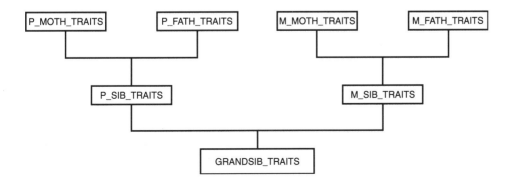

It is appropriate to use a family tree example when discussing inheritance and hierarchy, because this is the real-world example upon which this language process is based. This last example consists of the p_ and m_ (paternal and maternal) SIB_TRAITS classes that contain two bases. The GRANDSIB_TRAITS class is derived from the former two classes that, in turn, are each derived from two base classes. The inheritance of the GRANDSIB class eventually degenerates to four bases. This is certainly accurate in regard to the real-world nature of this discussion, because the grandchildren will tend to inherit traits of the four grandparents as well as the two parents. This structure has more than doubled in size over the original. Should a GREAT_GRANDSIB_TRAIT class be added, the structure would more than double again.

While the examples used in this block diagram are quite simple, it is readily apparent that inheritance can easily take on gigantic block proportions. The code that might be required for additional complex blocks (i.e., those that contain a fair number of data members and methods) would create a situation where the overall program would take on unwieldy proportions. The problem here is that it becomes increasingly difficult for the programmer to maintain a grasp of the code that makes up each block. C++ OOP methods do offer the black box effect, meaning that once a single class has been programmed, it may be treated as an entity with a personality, and the actual source code that has gone into this entity may be largely ignored.

This works well in theory, but practical application of this theory adds a few problems. One major difficulty is when a conflict arises between what the programmer planned to do and what may later be demanded. It is often necessary to go back to original class source code and make changes to address unanticipated tasks and problems. When dealing with a large, complex inheritance hierarchy, a change made within a lower class in the hierarchy usually mandates changes to all derived classes. It is for this reason that most practical object-oriented programs do not run to many tiers of hierarchy. As stated earlier, when a three-level inheritance is exceeded in all but the simplest of class constructions, maintaining the overall grasp of the program contents becomes very difficult.

Single-Instance Classes

To address some tasks, the programmer may find it desirable to build a class that has a single instance. This means that the class can be used to create only a single object. Two or more objects of this type are not possible. This is very easy to accomplish in C++ and borrows a similar type of formatting (tagging) as a one-instance struct in ANSI C. The following class is a single-instance type.

```
class {
    private:
        int x;
        double a;
    public:
        void assign(int i, double d)
        {

            x = i;
            a = d;

        }
        void display(void)
        {

            cout << x << "   " << a << endl;

        }

}
loner;    // single-instance object name
```

This class creates a single object with the tag **loner**. The name of the object is fixed, because this class has no name. No other objects may be created. It might be used in a C++ program in the following manner.

```
            int main()
            {

                loner.assign(4, 77.16);
                loner.display();

            }
```

Naturally, no declaration can be made, since the **loner** object is a single-instance type.

For simple classes with fixed-size intrinsic data members, this method works quite well due to its simplicity. However, one problem is that a single-instance class can have no constructor or destructor. Notice that a constructor was not a part of the class methods. Instead, the assign() method has been substituted. A constructor must have the same name as its class. The destructor has the same name as well, but is preceded by the tilde character (~). If a class has no name, then it is not possible for it to have a constructor and/or destructor. However, a single-instance class doesn't usually require (absolutely) a constructor or destructor since there will be no other objects of this type.

Creating Objects with New

The earlier discussions on polymorphism addressed accessing classes and class methods via pointers. It was noted that accessing a class method via a pointer required the use of the pointer to a member operator (->), whereas the member-of operator (.) is used when accessing local or global class members.

Carrying the discussion of pointer access farther, the **new** memory allocation operator can be used to create a class. The following program demonstrates this.

```
#include <iostream.h>
#include <string.h>
class employee {
    private:
        char *name;
        int empnum;
        double salary;
    public:
        employee(char *a, int x, double d)
        {
            name = new char[50];
            strcpy(name, a);
            empnum = x;
            salary = d;
        }
        ~employee(void)
        {

            delete name;
        }
```

```
            void display(void)
            {

                cout << empnum <<":" << name << " " << "has a
salary of $" << salary << endl;

            }
};
int main()
{

    employee *first_shift = new employee("Bill", 14,
280.65);

    first_shift->display();

    delete first_shift;

}
```

This program looks a bit strange, but when examined closely, it loses some of its alien appearance. There is nothing unusual about the class as it follows the standard format of previous class examples. The peculiarity shows up under main() where first_shift is declared a pointer of type **employee** and is then assigned to the line fragment below.

```
        new employee("Bill", 14, $280.65);
```

The new operator is called to set aside storage for the pointer. Such an operation means that the object is created on the *free store*. This is C++ jargon for the memory allocated by the new operator. The size of the storage is the size of the **employee** class. A class object has size just like an intrinsic int, double, char, or whatever. Storage is set aside in the amount needed for an object of type employee. At the same time, the constructor arguments are established. This program will display the following line on the monitor.

```
        14:Bill has a salary of $280.65
```

The familiar caveat "A pointer must always point to something" applies equally in C++ operations that create a pointer to a memory block using the **new** operator.

Certainly, an object of type employee could have been created along with a declared pointer of this same type. Through a separate operation the pointer could have been assigned the address of the object. However, this construct uses the **new** operator to set aside the required (free store) space for the pointer. This operator returns a pointer of the correct type and invokes the class constructor as well. Only a pointer to a class is being used, and all operations must be effected via the pointer-to-member operator. This is demonstrated by calling the display() method. The **delete** operator is used to destroy the object and the memory allocation that has occurred due to its creation.

Pointers and Polymorphism

By expanding the previous program example, the **new** operator can be used to access virtual functions in a hierarchy via the base class. The following program demonstrates this.

```
#include <iostream.h>
#include <string.h>
class employee {
    private:
        char *name;
        int empnum;
        double salary;
    public:
        employee(char *a, int x, double d)
        {
            name = new char[50];
            strcpy(name, a);
            empnum = x;
            salary = d;
        }
        ~employee(void)
        {

            delete name;

        }
        virtual void display(void)
        {

            cout << empnum <<":" << name << " " << "has a salary of " <<
salary << endl;

        }
```

```
};
class emp_record : public employee {
    private:
        char *title;
        int years_employed;
    public:
        emp_record(char *a, int x, double d, char *t, int ye) : employee(a, x, d)
        {

            title = new char[25];
            strcpy(title, t);
            years_employed = ye;

        }
        ~emp_record(void)
        {

            delete title;

        }
        void display(void)
        {

            employee::display();
            cout << "Employee's title is " << title << endl;
            cout << "Employed for " << years_employed << " years" << endl;

        }
};


int main()
{

    employee *first_shift = new emp_record("Bill", 14, 280.65, "Foreman", 22);

    first_shift->display();

    delete first_shift;

}
```

The class hierarchy in this example has been modified to include
a derived class (emp_record). The display() method under the base
class is declared virtual. Therefore, the display() method in the derived
class is also virtual (though not specifically declared as such), and either

may be accessed via the correct pointer assignment, as readers learned in the earlier discussions about polymorphism.

Under main(), first_shift is declared a pointer of type **employee**. Closely examine the assignment using the **new** operator. This operator is used in conjunction with the name of the derived class that also contains the constructor values. The end result is a base class pointer type that points to the derived class. When the following line of code is executed, the display() method contained within the derived class (emp_record) will be executed.

```
first_shift->display();
```

The resulting display is shown below.

```
14:Bill has a salary of $280.65
Employee's title is Foreman
Employed for 22 years
```

While this application seems to function properly, there is a definite problem that leads to another topic of discussion involving C++ classes and inheritance, that of destructors in derived classes.

Inheritance and Destructors

The previous program example works in a predictable manner, but there is a flaw that is inconsequential in this exact usage. However, this problem can cause many headaches when objects and programs take on real-world proportions. The problem lies with the destructors within this hierarchy.

In the last chapter, readers learned that base class constructors and destructors are not inherited by derived classes. The base class constructor must be specifically called by the inherited class constructor (shown above) by the derived class constructor code that follows.

```
emp_record(char *a, int x, double d, char *t, int ye) : employee(a, x, d)
{

    title = new char[25];
    strcpy(title, t);
    years_employed = ye;

}
```

Here, the constructor from the base class is called via the following extension.

```
: employee (a, x, d)
```

Therefore, the base class constructor is not inherited, but the derived class has access to this constructor, so it could be called. The same is true of destructors, and a destructor can fail to execute, given the correct set of circumstances.

The current program example provides the criteria necessary for just such a set of circumstances, and the derived class destructor (emp_record) *will not* be executed when the pointer is destroyed using the **delete** operator. The reason for this is that the derived class has been created by the **new** operator handing the address back to the base class pointer.

Since most destructors do not contain any type of screen prompt coding, the failure of the derived class destructor would not be noted. To see exactly what happens in the above program example, add the following code line to the end of the base class constructor

```
cout << "base class constructor executed" << endl;
```

and the following line to the end of the base class destructor.

```
cout << "base class destructor executed" << endl;
```

Next, add the following line to the end of the derived class constructor.

```
cout << "derived class constructor executed" << endl;
```

Finally, place the following line of code at the end of the derived class destructor.

```
cout << "derived class destructor executed" << endl;
```

These operations simply put screen prompts into each constructor and destructor so that their execution sequences can be visually monitored.

When this program is executed, the following sequence will appear on the screen.

```
base class constructor executed
derived class constructor executed
14:Bill has a salary of $280.65
Employee's title is Foreman
Employed for 22 years
base class destructor executed
```

It is clear that the base class constructor is executed first, followed by the derived class constructor. This is followed by the text display and then by the text line from the base class destructor. However, the derived class (emp_record) destructor was *never executed* and the memory allocated to the pointer named **title** has not been released.

This memory remains allocated, as it was not released by the **delete** operator as intended. In this simple example, the program ends immediately after the **delete** operator is used, so there is nothing to be concerned with from an execution point of view. However, if this program had been more complex and ran on after the **delete** operator was used, a problem with memory availability could result. Certainly 25 bytes of storage is not a premium amount in most modern microcomputers, but this amount could as easily have been 2.5 megabytes or even more in a practical application. Good programming practice requires that all allocated memory be released after it is no longer needed. This applies whether the allocated memory is 1 byte or 100 megabytes.

Fortunately, the solution to this problem is quite simple. The only change that needs to be made in the original program example is to declare the base class destructor as virtual. Constructors cannot be declared virtual, but there is no such limitation on destructors. Change the base class destructor opening line as follows.

```
virtual ~employee(void)
```

When the program is compiled and executed, it will display the following.

```
base class constructor executed
derived class constructor executed
14:Bill has a salary of $280.65
Employee's title is Foreman
```

```
Employed for 22 years
derived class destructor executed
base class destructor executed
```

Now, both destructors are executed when **delete** attempts to destroy the object. Since the base class *constructor* was executed first, the base class *destructor* is executed last. This is the proper chain of events that should take place.

The question now arises as to why making the base class destructor a virtual function brings about the execution of the derived class destructor. This is an exercise in (automatic) polymorphism.

Even though the base class destructor and the derived class destructor have different names, they both contain the same name as their respective classes. For this reason, they are treated (indirectly) as if they have the same name. If the base class destructor is declared virtual, then all derived class destructors are automatically virtual as well.

In this case alone the (destructor) function names don't matter. Even though access in the program example was gained only through the base class pointer, both destructors are now executed, and the same would be true of any number of additional classes that might be derived from the base.

It is enough to know that once a base class destructor has been declared virtual, it is certain that all derived class destructors will also be virtual and will be executed properly given any reasonable opportunity to do so. The problem of destructors not being executed does not apply to the more conventional uses of classes. However, when pointers to derived classes whose objects exist on the free store via the use of the **new** operator are involved, it is quite possible for the execution of a destructor to be omitted.

Many programmers automatically declare all base class destructors to be virtual, since it is impossible to predict how these classes will be utilized in the future. Through the virtual declaration, a safety factor is built into the class that can save unnecessary class body rewrites and/or hours of debugging.

A Practical Example of OOP

The first excursions of the (former) ANSI C programmer into practical C++ applications will most likely address the conversion of an existing C program to C++. Many ANSI C programs may not adapt well to OOP concepts and will best be left in their procedural-based formats. However, others will practically beg for an object-oriented makeover.

At the beginning of this book, the author attempted to convey a general idea of OOP using a pop-up window example. This discussion did not involve any actual source code, as its purpose was to provide an overview of the OOP process in practical terms. The journey from C to C++ has now come full circle, and it is appropriate to return to the pop-up window example, discussing it in terms of source code.

Graphics programs lend themselves well to object-oriented design because of the block aspect of most graphics images. Many computer graphic display programs can be easily broken down into different on-screen objects, a box here, a circle there, even a triangle. Each of these can become a discrete object within a C++ program, just as it is a discrete object on the screen.

While many tutorial examples of OOP start with a point (pixel) class and then build from there with a hierarchy of circles, squares, triangles, etc., the following example is more practical in that it begins with an ANSI C program used to produce text-mode pop-up windows and converts the function to a class that accomplishes the same thing in a fashion that makes the operation far more practical. This type of application was discussed theoretically in Chapter 1. The discussion now leaves the theoretical to deal with the actual code groups involved.

The initial ANSI C source code is for a function named popup() that produces a pop-up shadow window based on dimension values handed the function along with a duration value and text string that will appear in the window. This code was compiled using Borland Turbo C++, Version 3.0.

```
/* ANSI C function for pop-up windows */

void popup(int x, int y, int xx, int yy, int bg, int col,
int time, char *text)
{
    char far *c;
    int ct, q, mx, my, mxx, myy, hold[4000];
    mxx = xx;
    myy = yy;
    ct = 0;
    c = (char far *) 0xb8000000;

/* get original screen  */
```

```
    ct = 0;
    for( mx = x; mx <= mxx + 2; ++mx)
        for (my = y; my <= myy + 1; ++my) {
            q = ((mx - 1) * 2) + ((my - 1) * 160);
            hold[ct++] = *(c + q);
            hold[ct++] = *(c + q + 1);
        }

    _setcursortype(_NOCURSOR);

/* shadow window */
    window(x + 1, y + 1, xx + 2, yy + 1);
    textbackground(0);
    clrscr();

/* popup window */
    window(x, y, xx, yy);
    textbackground(bg);
    textcolor(col);
    clrscr();
    cprintf(text);

    sleep(time);

    _setcursortype(_NORMALCURSOR);

/* put back original screen */
    ct = 0;
    for( mx = x; mx <= mxx + 2; ++mx)
        for (my = y; my <= myy + 1; ++my) {
            q = ((mx - 1) * 2) + ((my - 1) * 160);
            *(c + q) = hold[ct++];
            *(c + q + 1) = hold[ct++];
        }



}
```

This function is broken down into four different parts. The first portion copies the screen segment that will be overwritten by the pop-up window prior to the window's being drawn. This is a simple screen dump routine that retains the original screen information in an array. Next, the shadow window is written. This is a black box matching the dimensions of the pop-up window, slightly offset to provide the shadow appearance.

The next block writes the actual window to the screen at the coordinates passed to the function during the initial call. When the window has been written on the screen, the text string is written. The sleep() function is used to maintain the window for a certain number of seconds (also supplied as an argument). When this function times out, the last block rewrites the original screen, thus erasing the pop-up window and returning the screen to its original condition.

The arguments to the function are listed below.

```
x,y        = upper left edge of window
xx, yy     = lower right edge of window
bg         = box background color
col        = text write color
time       = duration of window
*text      = text string to be written in window
```

The function has been written in such a manner that, once it begins executing, nothing else occurs until it completes its run and returns control to the calling program. It is useful for displaying a brief message in a pop-up window on the screen.

However, there is a major limitation in that only one pop-up window at a time may appear on the screen, assuming that this is the only function used for generating such windows. When popup() is executing, nothing else can happen until the window has been established, filled with text, and then erased.

In order to add versatility, assume that this function is to be changed in a manner that would allow it to establish the window and the message and then be removed (at some later point) by a separate function. This presents a few problems in that it would be necessary to call a separate function first that would copy the current screen contents where the window is to appear. This would be followed by the function that would actually write the pop-up window (and the shadow window). Finally, a third function would be required that would erase the window by overwriting it with the original screen information.

There are some added difficulties. For example, each of the three functions would necessarily have to have the same coordinate information. The third function would also need the address of the array that holds the initial screen information. Because of these complexities, such an operation is best addressed in an object-oriented manner, where each window becomes an object, one that is written and erased by methods of the class that forms that object.

The following class structure addresses all of these features in a very straightforward and simple manner. Much of the original source code from popup() has been retained in writing the methods of this class. Since the window will be written by one operation and erased by another, no time value is needed, and the sleep() function can be eliminated. The class source code is shown below.

```
class popup {
    private:
        char far *c, *text;
        int x, y, xx, yy, bg, col, hold[4000];
    public:
        popup(int ix, int iy, int ixx, int iyy, int ibg, int icol, char *itext)
        {

            x = ix;
            y = iy;
            xx = ixx;
            yy = iyy;
            bg = ibg;
            col = icol;
            text = new[200];
            strcpy(text, itext);
            c = (char far *) 0xb8000000;

        }
        ~popup()
        {

            delete c;
            delete text;

        }
        void make_win(void)    //Make the pop-up window
        {

        // get original screen
        int ct = 0;
        for(int mx = x; mx <= xx + 2; ++mx)
```

```
        for (int my = y; my <= yy + 1; ++my) {
            int q = ((mx - 1) * 2) + ((my - 1) * 160);
            hold[ct++] = *(c + q);
            hold[ct++] = *(c + q + 1);
        }

    _setcursortype(_NOCURSOR);

//shadow window
    window(x + 1, y + 1, xx + 2, yy + 1);
    textbackground(0);
    clrscr();

//popup window
    window(x, y, xx, yy);
    textbackground(bg);
    textcolor(col);
    clrscr();
    cprintf(text);

    _setcursortype(_NORMALCURSOR);

}
void rem_win(void)    // Remove the pop-up window
{

    //put back original screen
    int ct = 0;
    for(int mx = x; mx <= xx + 2; ++mx)
        for (int my = y; my <= yy + 1; ++my) {
            int q = ((mx - 1) * 2) + ((my - 1) * 160);
            *(c + q) = hold[ct++];
            *(c + q + 1) = hold[ct++];
        }
}

};
```

The various source code blocks that were discussed previously can be readily discerned. The class contains two methods called make_win() and rem_win() that make and remove the window, respectively. There is no problem in having to pass addresses back and forth between different entities as would be the case if functions were involved in effecting this operation in a procedural-based manner. This also means that each pop-up window is a true object and a programmer may use as many as desired when manipulating such objects within a C++ program.

The following C++ program provides a simple demonstration of how this class may be used to create two pop-up windows on the screen.

```
#include <stdlib.h>
#include <conio.h>
#include <string.h>
#include <popup.h>
#include <dos.h>
#include <iostream.h>

int main()
{

    system("DIR/w");

    popup win1(3, 5, 20, 8, 1, 3, "\r\n\nFirst Window Write\r\n");
    popup win2(25, 20, 45, 22, 2, 1, "\r\n Second Window Write\r\n");

    win1.make_win();
    win2.make_win();

    getch();

    win2.rem_win();

    getch();

    win1.rem_win();

}
```

This simple program uses the system() function to send the **DIR**ectory command (**DIR**)to DOS, which will list the contents of the current direc-tory in a wide format (/w). Next, two objects of type **popup** are created. The popup class is found in the popup.h header file that is #included at the beginning of the program.

There are two pop-up window objects named win1 and win2. The next two calls utilize the make_win() class method. This means that the two windows will be created on the screen. The calls to getch() provide temporary execution halts. When a key is pressed, the second window will seem to disappear as its screen area is overwritten with the information that was found there originally, prior to the window being written. Pressing another key will result in the first window being overwritten by original screen information. At this point, the screen will appear exactly as it did prior to writing the first pop-up window.

The reader should be able to see immediately the benefit that an object-oriented approach has brought to this type of application. It is no longer necessary to think of each pop-up window as a set of screen coordinates. Rather, each window now has its own name, such as win1 and win2, although they might just as easily have been named Bob and Bill.

The win1 object creates itself, assigns itself, and destroys itself. The same operational criteria apply to win2. Each window is a separate object, controlled by itself. There is no longer any concern about address swapping, overwrites, and the like. The windows are programmed in the same fashion they are viewed by humans—as physical objects.

To gain a better grasp of the OOP process, compare the object-oriented manner in which text windows are written with the ANSI C function counterpart. This is a necessary comparison because, initially, many C programmers have difficulty in understanding the advantage OOP has over ANSI C functions.

Initially, the C function created only a single type of pop-up window, one that was of limited duration and that required a duration time argument. This was necessary because the screen area where the window was to appear had to be captured before the window was written. Later, the window was made to disappear by rewriting the original screen contents at this window location. The basis for converting this function into a C++ class was the desire to be able to program two or more pop-up windows that would appear simultaneously on the screen and could be destroyed by separate program commands. To accomplish this via ANSI C functions would require at least two and probably three or more functions. Also necessary would be some global variables that keep track of the number of windows present and other global variables that give a separate identity to each window created. All these steps, variables, and functions would be necessary in ANSI C to give each window a separate identity. Treating each window as a unique object was the purpose all along, even though the ANSI C programmer would probably be unaware of such a goal, at least in those terms.

C++ makes it far easier to accomplish this goal. Readers must understand that the ANSI C popup() function can create only (in OOP terminology) a single object. If we wish to create ten objects, then we must call the function ten times. Even then, ten separate objects are not created. Using OOP terminology, the same object is created on ten different occasions. Even though the size, text contents, and color of each window might be different, each window is still the same object.

Using the C++ class construct, we may create any number of separate objects, all at the same time if desired. Certainly, each window is an object of type popup. However, each window is also a discrete object. There is no relationship between any two windows of type popup, just as there is no interaction relationship between a Chevrolet Corvette in California and one in New York. They are the same type of automobile, they may even be the same color and configuration, but they are discrete objects, separate physical entities of the same type. This means that if one car is to be used for racing purposes, the other need not be. Each automobile may be used uniquely. The same applies to the pop-up windows created by this class.

In the previous program example, each window is given its own name. What is done with one window need not be done with the other. Certainly, there are limitations as to what any window of this type can do, but within these limitations there are many operational variables that can be used to advantage to create many discrete entities that are of the same type but that operate independently and uniquely.

Using ANSI C functions, only one object (again, in OOP terminology) can be created. Perhaps it is created many times, but it is still the same object. Through C++, we may create any number of separate objects, and each may be treated as a discrete entity. This manner of programming reflects the real world and offers many advantages that provide far more power for most tasks than a procedural-based approach.

Minor Alterations to an Existing Program

The reader has now been presented with the tools for OOP in C++ and has a good working knowledge of how they are used. At this point in the journey from C to C++, it is appropriate to discuss the general methods by which typical programming problems can be addressed, overcome, or avoided within a C++ environment.

Even the best preprogram planning will not address all of the potential needs a complex task requires. Programmers commonly need to make some minor change in what has already been programmed to address an unforeseen need. What is the best way to proceed in such instances?

Assume that the task element that is not currently addressed represents a minor problem that requires a minor change in the source code as it currently exists. For example, assume that a C++ program has been written that, among other things, stores the last word in each line of text in a multidimensional character array. Suddenly, it is discovered that the capability of storing the first word in each line in a separate character array is also needed.

A method already exists that detects, retrieves, and then stores the last word in each text line. This is close to what is needed for the new operation; therefore, the new tool does not differ much from the old tool.

There is one safe rule of thumb in such circumstances: Don't alter what already works. By making certain changes in one class, it is possible that derived classes and/or other program elements may be adversely affected. Many professional programmers lament the time that they had a program on the verge of completion and then made one little change to existing source code that resulted in many hours of troubleshooting. Simple changes are often the most damaging. These can result in simple auxiliary problems that are, in turn, addressed by more simple changes. Sometimes, the end result is an attempt to get back to square one, the point at which the first minor change was made.

The ideal method of addressing the need for a minor change in a program involving (especially) a complex class hierarchy is to develop a new class to address the extra operations. This means that there will be effectively no changes to existing program structure. The new class is simply tacked on to the original code to address a specific need.

Certainly, some might say that this is bad programming, using a band-aid fix for a situation that should have been anticipated. The purist would require the programmer to go back to the beginning and rewrite the program to address all tasks right from the start. In the real world, however, this is a waste of time and effort. If a simple, obvious fix can be made by adding a new, not-so-complex class, then do so.

Another solution might be found in the form of a friend function. Chapter 5 explained that this type of function is not a member of a class but still has full access to all class members, specifically the data members. While it is true that the overuse of friend functions tends to destroy the object-oriented approach, prudent use of them is recommended, especially for patching of the type under discussion. Friend functions have been described as a window of procedural-based programming in an object-oriented environment. Again, the purists might object, but the whole purpose of OOP is to offer the programmer more flexibility along with increased programming power.

If reverting to procedural-based mode occasionally adds flexibility and power, then use it. One is reminded of the **goto** statement in ANSI C. It has always been considered poor programming practice to use this statement because it tends to destroy program structure. However, it exists for a multitude of reasons, and one of them is to provide a quick and dirty method of jumping over a troublesome (and structured) program segment or to jump back to a point that should have been addressed by proper looping using **while**, **for**, or **do-while** statements. The goto statement is present because human programmers will make procedural errors that are best corrected in a practical manner—by a patch as opposed to a complete rewrite. In some ways, a C++ friend function may be used in the same fashion.

Programmers still must realize that the overuse of friend functions or using them to make up for a sloppy preplanning regimen is to be avoided at all costs. Bear in mind that the general type of problem under discussion assumes that the program is well under way or almost completed and only a minor change is required.

Adding a new derived class is not always the *best* answer. As a rule, if the necessary changes can be effected by means of a friend function, then do so. If the needed changes are so small that they affect only a line or two of a single class in the hierarchy (and not its interaction with other classes), then this would seem to be the best avenue. If the changes would involve altering several classes in different ways, then derive another class to avoid making them. In short, if changes to the current class architecture would alter the personality of the class in a major way (i.e., change the general way the class works), then the new derived class is clearly the best choice. If the changes to existing classes only make them more efficient but still allow them to do the same thing, then make the changes to the existing class structure.

There are no hard and fast rules to changing an existing class hierarchy. Different situations will require different solutions. The ways and means outlined in this chapter are meant to serve as a rough, general guide in how to proceed. In many situations, it may be necessary to use a combination of these suggestions to address most efficiently the changes.

C++ Names and Identifiers

It has become an ANSI C tradition to use (with few exceptions) only lower-case letters in writing programs. Many reasons are given for this, including the inability of the original MS-DOS linker to differentiate between upper- and lower-case function names. However, the main reason is probably programming speed, in that it is rarely necessary to press the Shift key to access the upper-case alphabet. This does tend to speed things up but sometimes at the cost of program clarity.

At present there is no standard for C++ identifiers. Most C programmers making the switch to C++ continue to program in the standard, lower-case fashion. Those who have entered C++ from other language environments that encourage a mixed-case form of identifier notation will probably carry this style over into C++. For the present, the goal of any programmer should be to write source code that is easy to understand. This is a subjective goal that will be defined in many different ways.

As a rule of thumb, the ANSI C tradition of using upper-case for #define constants will suffice nicely for C++. Most variable names and function names will still be in lower case.

However, the naming of classes is definitely progressing toward a mixed-case format. An ANSI C struct might be named as follows.

```
sort_list_ascending
```

On the other hand, a C++ class would normally utilize a mixed-case notation as shown below.

```
SortListAscending
```

In this example, an upper-case letter is used to begin each field of the class name. C++ is still a relatively new language, but programmers have taken to using this mixed-case method for naming class methods as well. This style has become an unofficial standard.

The exact method used in naming identifiers, for now, is largely a matter of programmer preference and hinges mostly on the language base from which that programmer has entered C++. The reader is aware by now that C++ source code quickly takes on very large proportions, much more so than would be the case with an equivalent (non-OOP) ANSI C program. As a result, maintaining source code clarity is of paramount importance.

The clarity alluded to is not necessarily directed toward programmers who must read source code written by someone else (although this is a strong consideration where team efforts are involved). Rather, the clarity must be maintained so that the authoring programmer will continue to have a handle on what has taken place when writing his or her own source code. The simple examples throughout this book do not adequately emphasize the ease with which programmers may become lost in their own source code. With this in mind, the programmer must establish a set of identifier naming rules that he or she adheres to at all times. Failing this, lack of source code clarity will certainly result in many hours of wasted debugging time due, simply, to a lack of understanding of what has already been written.

Class Organization

The examples in this text have placed the code for the various classes within the calling program source code—i.e., the entire program has been contained in a single file. While this method lends itself well to instructional purposes, it will rarely be followed in practical programming applications.

Most often, class definitions will be contained in a separate header file that will be #included with the main() program portion. While the exact nature and complexity of any one class will be a determinant, most programmers favor the convention of segregating each class within its own separate header file. This is often modified when closely linked derived classes are involved. In such instances, a single class hierarchy will be contained in each header file.

Summary

Readers can see that classes may be combined through inheritance hierarchies in almost any conceivable manner. Inheritance can be handled in a straight-line, pyramidal manner, springing from a single base class. Alternately, these hierarchies may be built from two or more base classes, both of which pass on their properties to all derived classes. Access to data members and/or member functions is controlled via the private, protected, and public access specifiers. This allows fine-tuning of derived classes regarding which portions of their base classes may be freely accessed.

While class hierarchies take on gigantic proportions at times, practical limitations are usually applied that restrict inheritance to three or four levels at the most, although you may see this practice ignored in certain applications, especially those that address artificial intelligence. Once inheritance passes beyond a three-tiered hierarchy, it becomes more difficult to maintain a handle on all of the processes that can take place.

This chapter has highlighted some of the differences between typical ANSI C approaches and the C++ approach to the same task. It has also served to show that there need not be a complete difference in coding, as most of the code originally found in the ANSI C sample functions was retained within the C++ class member functions used for an object-oriented approach to addressing a task. The main difference is one of conceptualization and implementation. In converting current ANSI C applications to C++, the programmer must first ask, "Does the task(s) being addressed lend itself to an OOP approach?" The answer will be based on an ability to divide the task elements into separate entities or objects. If this is desirable, then there should be little difficulty involved in making the changes a step at a time.

Using the simple pop-up window generator as an example, there is clearly a decided advantage in segregating each window into the category of a separate object (all of the same type). Once the conversion had been accomplished, the on-screen windows ceased to be identical entities. Rather, each became a unique entity with its own name and operational characteristics, although limited by the personality of the popup class, proper. All windows had something in common regarding description and operation, but each was controlled and manipulated in an object-oriented fashion.

This final chapter dealt with a number of diverse subjects, all of which relate in some form or other to program design considerations. Many of these might be classified as the hints-and-tips portion of the journey from C to C++. As experience with C++ programming increases, many other useful tips and shortcuts will be discovered and used to make future programs even more versatile and efficient.

This journey from C to C++ is now complete, but don't assume there is nothing left to learn or that you are now a professional C++ programmer. There are many other aspects to this language and to OOP that are yet to be experienced, and the learning process will continue as long as you continue to write programs.

The materials in this book have been presented in a manner that is designed to answer the most-asked questions about C++. If you have absorbed the discussions and examples, then you will have established a base from which marvelous new discoveries will spring. Through continued efforts at "thinking" the object-oriented approach and committing such ideas to working C++ programs, your capabilities will expand to even higher levels.

Index

Other Academic Press Titles of Interest

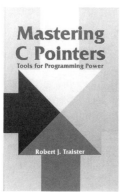

The Complete C++ Primer, Second Edition
by Keith Weiskamp and Bryan Flamig

This new edition of the popular hands-on guide to C++ programming provides an easy way to help you master C++. Let noted authors Keith Weiskamp and Bryan Flamig show you how to use the important features of C++ Version 2.1, inlcuding classes, functions, constructors and destructors, stream I/O, operator overloading, inheritance, and more. You'll also find coverage of the new template features.

ISBN 0-12-742686-8 $34.95

Introductory C: Pointer, Functions, and Files
by Richard Petersen

C differs from most programming languages in its use of pointers, functions, and files. For those learning C, pointers are the greateset source of confusion. The primary aim of this text is to provide working models of how pointers are used in C. The book provides clear and simple programs to highlight each new feature of C. The primary focus is on what a programmer needs to know in order to get a program running.

ISBN 0-12-552140-5 $34.95

Mastering C Pointers: Tools for Programming Power
by Robert J. Traister

If you don't fully understand pointers and how they are used, then you really don't know how to program in C. This book was written to take the mystery out of C pointers by explaining exactly what they are in plain language and illustrating their use in easy-to-follow examples.

Unleash the full power of the C language with a thorough knowledge of pointers and their use! Both newcomers and veteran C programmers will find this book an essential addition to their set of C programming tools.

ISBN 0-12-697408-X $45.00

Other Academic Press Titles of Interest

Learning C with Fractals
by Roger Stevens

Learn to program in C while generating beautiful fractals!

Learning C with Fractals is the first introductory level book to use exciting, graphical programs and fractals to teach the tools for programming in C. If you've had a little programming experience, but are unfamiliar with C, you can now learn all the skills necessary to become an expert C programmer while producing beautiful fractal pictures rather than simple text sample programs. This book covers all of the major versions of C compilers and introduces the key features of C programming, which you practice with graphics and fractal programs. All of the colorful fractals introduced in the book can be generated easily, with short, easy-to-understand programs.

The example programs in this book are designed to run on an IBM PC or clone with a VGA card and monitor. The book also shows you how to modify the programs so that they will work with an EGA card and monitor. The programs were developed using Borland C++, but will also work with Turbo C, Turbo C++, MicroSoft C, MicroSoft C++, Zortec C++, or Power C compilers.

ISBN 0-12-668315-8 $44.95

The C Graphics Handbook
by Roger T. Stevens

Programming graphics in C is made easy with *The C Graphics Handbook*. This handbook contains all of the tools needed to set up display modes for EGA, VGA, or Super VGA cards. It also covers three-dimensional drawing techniques using C and C++, and provides programs for saving display screens to disk files and restoring screens using the common compression formats PCX, IMG, and GIF. Also includes a disk for IBM and compatibles containing all of the code from the text.

ISBN 0-12-668320-4 $39.95

Other Academic Press Titles of Interest

The Graphics Gems Series
Series editor, Andrew Glassner

This three volume series is a collection of carefully crafted gems which offer techniques, ideas, tools, and tricks that capture the spirit of the creative graphics programmer and represent the diversity in the graphics community today. Each volume contains completely new and innovative gems that are immediately accessible and useful in formulating clean, fast, and elegant programs. All of the gems are written by members of the graphics community, and provide a wide variety of approaches that can be used to find solutions to specific problems or as the starting point for new projects. All of the source code for the first three volumes of *Graphics Gems* is included on a disk accompanying Volume III. A number of the images generated through these algorithms are included in color inserts in all three volumes.

Volume I	ISBN 0-12-286165-5	$49.95
Volume II	ISBN 0-12-064480-0	$49.95
Volume III	ISBN 0-12-409670-0 (IBM)	$49.95
	ISBN 0-12-409671-9 (MAC)	$49.95

Virtual Reality: Applications and Explorations
by Alan Wexelblat

The ability of computers to store and manipulate vast amounts of data has made it possible to create worlds made out of pure information, drastically redefining the human-computer interface. *Virtual Reality: Applications and Expolorations* collects original essays that examine a broad range of practical applications of virtual reality, from entertainment and architectural design to teleconferencing and computer-supported cooperative work. Researchers at the forefront of work in this area explain the capabilities of some present systems and outline the even more compelling possibilities they envision.

ISBN 0-12-745-45-9 $34.95 (tentative)

Other Academic Press Titles of Interest

Practical Neural Network Recipes in C++
by Timothy Masters

This text is a practical guide to neural network solutions using C++. It enables those with moderate programming experience to select an appropriate neural network model for solving a particular problem, and to produce a working program for implementing that network. No background in neural networks is assumed and all models are presented from the ground up. Also includes a diskette for IBM and compatibles containing the source code for all programs in the book.

ISBN 0-12-489040-2 $44.95

Image Processing Using C
by Christopher D. Watkins and Alberto Sadun

Image Processing has applications to numerous disciplines, and with the availability of powerful and inexpensive hardware, it is now an area being implemented and investigted by all levels of computer users. *Image Processing Using C* contains both practical and theoretical information regarding techniques for processing images that are scanned or taken through a CCD (camera arrays-digital cameras). It instructs the reader about how to enhance, manipulate, and extract information from the images which have been acquired. The book also includes the source code required to perform all of the image manipulation.

ISBN 0-12-737860-X $49.95 (tentative)

Multimedia Production Handbook for the IBM PC,
Macintosh, and Amiga
by Tom Yager

This handbook is a comprehensive resource guide for selecting an appropriate multimedia system from among the many currently available. It focuses on three of the best platforms for Multimedia applications: IBM, Macintosh, and Amiga. Author Tom Yager brings 2 years of experience as director of *Byte Magazine's* Multimedia Lab to this exciting new text. By using this book, managers, developers, and end-users can more effectively map out their time and capital for resources and development.

ISBN 0-12-768030-6 $39.95 (tentative)

ORDER FORM

To Order: Return this form with your payment to Academic Press, Order Fulfillment Department, 6277 Sea Harbor Drive, Orlando, FL 32821-9816, or **call toll-free 1-800-321-5068.**

QUANTITY	AUTHOR/TITLE	ISBN	PRICE

Subtotal	
Sales Tax (where applicable)	
TOTAL	

☐ Payment enclosed (please include applicable tax)
☐ Bill me directly (We cannot ship to a P.O. box)*
☐ Bill my company (purchase order attached)*
   *Shipping, handling, and tax will be added to billed orders. Tax will be added to credit card orders.

Charge card #_____ Expiration Date _____

Your Signature _____

Name_____ Telephone_____

Address _____

City_____ State/Country_____

Zip/Postal Code_____